Frameworks for Integrated Project-Based Instruction in STEM Disciplines

A Volume in Research, Innovation, &
Methods in Educational Technology

Series Editors

Chrystalla Mouza
University of Illinois Urbana-Champaign
Nancy C. Lavigne
University of Delaware

Research, Innovation, & Methods in Educational Technology

Chrystalla Mouza and Nancy C. Lavigne, Series Editors

Frameworks for Integrated Project-Based Instruction in STEM Disciplines (2024)
By Anthony J. Petrosino, Candace Walkington, and Denise Ekberg

Professional Development for In-Service Teachers Professional Development for In-Service Teachers (2022)
edited by Chrystalla Mouza, Anne Ottenbreit-Leftwich, and Aman Yadav

Preparing Pre-Service Teachers to Teach Computer Science: Models, Practices, and Policies (2021)
edited by Chrystalla Mouza, Chrystalla Mouza, and Anne Ottenbreit-Leftwich

Research on Technology in English Education (2013)
edited by Carl A. Young and Sara Kajder

Evaluating Technology in Teacher Education: Lessons From the Preparing Tomorrow's Teachers for Technology (PT3) Program (2010)
edited by Walt Heinecke and Pete Adamy

Research on Technology in Social Studies Education (2009)
edited by John Lee and Adam M. Friedman

Constructivist Instructional Design (C-ID): Foundations, Models, and Examples (2009)
edited by Jerry W. Willis

Evaluating Electronic Portfolios in Teacher Education (2009)
edited by Pete Adamy and Natalie B. Milman

Framing Research on Technology and Student Learning in the Content Areas: Implications for Educators (2008)
edited by Lynn Bell, Lynne Schrum, and Ann D. Thompson

Qualitative Research Methods in Education and Educational Technology (2008)
by Jerry W. Willis

Faculty Development by Design: Integrating Technology in Higher Education (2007)
edited by Punya Mishra, Matthew J. Koehler, and Yong Zhao

Faculty Mentoring: The Power of Students in Developing Technology Expertise (2007)
edited by Ann D. Thompson, Hsueh-Hua Chuang, and Ismail Sahin

Series titles continue on next page

Technology and Assessment:
The Tale of Two Interpretations (2006)
edited by Michael Russell

What Should Teachers Know about Technology:
Perspectives and Practices (2003)
edited by Yong Zhao

Methods of Evaluating Educational Technology (2001)
edited by Walt Heinecke and Laura Blasi

Frameworks for Integrated Project-Based Instruction in STEM Disciplines

By

Anthony J. Petrosino
*The University of Texas at Austin
and Southern Methodist University*

Candace Walkington
Southern Methodist University

Denise Ekberg
UTeach Natural Sciences

INFORMATION AGE PUBLISHING, INC.
Charlotte, NC • www.infoagepub.com

Library of Congress Cataloging-in-Publication Data

CIP record for this book is available from the Library of Congress
http://www.loc.gov

ISBNs: 979-8-88730-367-3 (Paperback)

979-8-88730-368-0 (Hardcover)

979-8-88730-369-7 (ebook)

Copyright © 2024 Information Age Publishing Inc.

All rights reserved. No part of this publication may be reproduced, stored in a retrieval system, or transmitted, in any form or by any means, electronic, mechanical, photocopying, microfilming, recording or otherwise, without written permission from the publisher.

Printed in the United States of America

CONTENTS

Preface .... *ix*

Acknowledgments .... *xi*

1. What Is PBI *1*
2. Linking the History of the "Project Method" to Current PBI Movements *17*
3. Six Major Elements of PBI *35*
4. Putting Your Project Together *85*
5. PBI Across Engineering, Computer Science, and Mathematics ... *111*
6. Practical Implementation of PBI at Scale: Administration and Assessment *133*
7. The Future of PBI Curricula: Issues of Technology and Community *149*

About the Authors *165*

PREFACE

Frameworks for Integrated Project-Based Instruction in STEM Disciplines offers in- depth information about the fundamental aspects of Project-based instruction and research-based strategies for implementing the approach.

This book is intended to unify theory with practice, covering information from major research on project-based instruction (PBI) as well as providing sample projects and planning tools for teachers. Specifically, this book contains deep coverage of four topics in PBI: scaffolding, student-driven inquiry, driving questions, and development of lessons based on national and state standards. The goal of this work is to provide readers with a deep understanding of PBI, which will present readers with tools that allow them to create strong and meaningful lesson experiences for their students. This book highlights the importance of thorough scaffolding throughout lessons, where every piece added to a project is an important step in steering the lesson towards learning goals. An emphasis on student-driven inquiry is discussed, including the importance of giving students the cognitive tools they need in order to research and inquire, such as those involved in statistical analysis. The components of a successful driving question are explained in detail, and examples are provided. Additionally, the book includes a description of the process of breaking apart and elaborating on national and state standards to develop curricula. This work is strongly rooted in research in the learning sciences about project-based instruction, but it is also designed to be practically useful to teachers as well as teacher educators and researchers by bridging research and practice.

Our ideas about PBI are based directly on both our experiences as K–12 STEM educators and our experiences as teacher-educators as part of the UTeach Program. The UTeach program is a secondary STEM teaching certification program that was founded at the University of Texas at Austin in 1992. It is based on the principle that teacher candidates need deep content knowledge, deep knowledge of pedagogy, and a nuanced understanding of how pedagogy and content come together to inform teaching decisions in secondary STEM. The UTeach program has been widely replicated and is currently offered at 45 different universities. The program was founded to aggressively recruit science, technology, engineering, and mathematics (STEM) majors into teaching careers, to allow them to get a full STEM major with teaching credentials in four years, and to prepare them to used research-based strategies anchored in the learning sciences in their classrooms, such as project-based instruction.

Project-based instruction (PBI) is the capstone course in the sequence of professional development courses (knowing and learning, classroom interactions, and PBI) that UTeach students take prior to their student teaching. A major focus of the PBI course is on designing, implementing, and evaluating problem-based and project-based learning approaches. The content of this course emerged from collaborations between teachers and researchers. Skills in integrating the STEM disciplines and STEM-specific pedagogical content knowledge are developed as UTeach students work toward the design of project-based units.

PBI is the course in which a number of the major principles and themes of the UTeach program—integration of mathematics and science content; infusion of technology in representation, analysis, modeling, assessment and contextualization of content; immersion in intensive field-based experiences; and a focus on designing equitable learning environments—are synthesized as the students develop an intellectually challenging project-based instructional unit. Competency is continually built as students read about and discuss the principles of PBI; reflect on observations of project-based learning environments in high school settings; and incorporate what they are learning into the design of inquiry-based lessons, and ultimately, an entire project-based unit. An intensive field component includes observation of well-implemented PBI in local schools as well as implementation of inquiry-based lessons with area high school students in an out-of-classroom field setting.

PBI is a key component of the UTeach professional development sequence and is based on the premise that PBI engages learners in exploring authentic, important, and meaningful questions of real concern to students.

ACKNOWLEDGMENTS

This endeavor would never have been possible without the help of hundreds of dedicated and talented individuals. First, we thank the teachers and students who have worked with us to test and refine many of the lessons and activities included in this book. The opportunity to work with them has been the highlight of our work. Confidentiality requirements mean we cannot list them by name, but we thank them deeply for their commitment and service, especially those from Ben Franklin High School in New Orleans (1992–2005).

Much of this book would not have been possible without grant support from several important agencies. A National Aeronautics and Space Administration Fellowship and Space Grant Consortium grant provided early support in the area of generative design and a grant from the James s. McDonnell Foundation via their Cognitive Studies in Educational Practice (CSEP) program provided funding for work in the area of middle school students understanding of experimentation and variation. The National Science Foundation funded work in the area of anchored instruction (NSF-MDR-9252990) as well as early support for the UTeach Program (DUE-9953187). It was this NSF support that led to the creation of the original Project-Based Instruction course. Related research in the area of K–16 engineering education for professional development (NSF-DRL-0831811), for the development of curriculum and associated research on curricula effectiveness in biomedical education (NSF-EEC-9876363), and for integrated methods of projects in robotics for STEM workforce development (NSF-DRL-0833726) and underrepresented youth (NSF-DRL-1615207) have also benefited from National Science Foundation and has contributed to this work. We are extremely grateful for all of this support. Nevertheless,

---

Frameworks for Integrated Project-Based Instruction in STEM Disciplines, pp. xi–xiii
Copyright © 2024 by Information Age Publishing
www.infoagepub.com
All rights of reproduction in any form reserved.

the ideas expressed in this book reflect our opinions, not the opinions of the grant agencies.

Thank you to the leadership at The University of Texas at Austin and Southern Methodist University. One cannot imagine a more supportive and encouraging environment in which to produce this volume.

To our original advisors and mentors, we owe our appreciation and our gratitude. Among these scholars are Rick Duschl, Susan R. Goldman, Richard Lehrer, Mitch Nathan, James Pellegrino, Bob Sherwood and the late John D. Bransford. We are deeply indebted and remain in awe and indebted to your intellect, grace, generosity, and humanity.

Special acknowledgements to the members of our extended communities of practice, those who provided meaningful conversations, resources, suggestions … and whose own work in the area was influential in the formation of some of our own ideas and who provided encouraging words and support during the life of this project: Flavio Azevedo, Brigid Barron, Phillip Bell, Janet Bowers, Corey Brady, Sean Brophy, Monica Cox, Richard Crawford, Carol Dickson, Barry Fishman, Elice Forman, Ricki Goldman, Ted Hasselbring, Tom Harris, Daniel Hickey, Cindy Hmelo, Stephanie Knight, Matt Koehler, Joe Krajcik, Victor Lee, Beth McGrath, Ann McKenna, Joyce Moore, Chandra Muller, Roy Pea, William "Bill" Penuel, Jay Pfaffman, Joe Polman, Brian Reiser, Bill Sandoval, Dan Schwartz, Janie Schielack, Bruce Sherin, Diana Sharp, Ada Stein, Barry Stein, Walter Stroup, Keisha Varma, Sashank Varma, Uri Wilensky and Michelle Wilkerson.

We are thankful to those to read early versions of some of these chapters and provided meaningful feedback and comments: Teddy Chao, Margaret Lucero, Michele Mann, Marc Sager, and Maximilian Sherard.

Special thank you to Jennifer Cook and Kasi Holcomb-Webb for their professional expertise in reviewing and revising content for accuracy and quality, including spelling, grammar, punctuation, and syntax as well as helping with correct tone, voice, clarity, flow and structure of content.

We are grateful to the editors of this book, Nancy Lavigne and Chrystalla Mouza. Each have provided substantive feedback and suggestions along the way and their stewardship has been invaluable. We would like to thank them for having faith in this project, for their patience, and for the extra effort they put into this volume. Both individually and as a team, their influence and stewardship has had nothing but a positive impact on this work. We would also like to thank George Johnson, the founder and publisher of Information Age Publishing, and staff for their efforts in making this endeavor a reality.

Words cannot fully express our gratitude to our UTeach Natural Sciences colleagues at The University of Texas at Austin. What began as an attempt to merge deep disciplinary knowledge, practical real world teaching expertise, and the latest research in the learning sciences has become a nationally recognized university-based teacher education program. Funding from the Howard Hughes Foundation, Exxon Mobil, AT&T, and the National Science Foundation as well as support from the National Math and Science Initiative has assisted in UTeach being replicated at more than 45 sites around the country. While there are many people to recognize, we would like to thank long time Codirectors Larry Abraham, Jill Marshall, and Michael Marder along with Kelli Allen, Flavio Azevedo, Deanna Buckley, Jere Confrey, Catherine Riegle-Crumb, Gail Dickenson, Pamela Garrison Elias, Lynn Kirby, Shelly Rodriguez, Victor Sampson, Mary Walker and the Director of the UTeach Institute Kim Hughes for all their effort and support with this volume.

Finally, we would like to acknowledge appreciation to family and close friends who have been through this process all the way from the initial thoughts of putting this work together into a volume, to the hours of reading, writing and providing both encouragement and times of welcomed and needed distraction: Aldo Fazio, Wendell Jamieson, Henry Lin, Linda Partoll, Mike Mapes, Concetta Drew-Petrosino, John Petrosino, Joseph Popovich, Karen and Frank Raia, Phil Ruden, Sarah Goff Raslowsky, Jennifer Hindman Sargent, John Raslowsky II, David Settembre, Paul and Amanda Spagnoletti, Helene Stapinski and Pat Steiner (*in memoriam*).

All of us owe debts of gratitude to those in our personal lives who support our professional careers with patience, care, love, and understanding. For me, the person who fills this role is Stacey Shackelford who shows me daily what understanding is and what it means to be supportive and encouraging in our lives together.

—Anthony J. Petrosino Jr

CHAPTER 1

WHAT IS PBI?

INTEGRATED STEM INSTRUCTION

When considering and defining project-based instruction (PBI) in the context of science, technology, engineering, and mathematics (STEM) teaching, a foundational idea is that of STEM itself—what it means and what it looks like. Thus, we begin this volume by briefly discussing STEM education more generally and then move into a discussion of PBI.

STEM is an acronym that refers to the academic and professional disciplines of science, technology, engineering, and mathematics. The term is usually used when discussing education policy and curriculum choices in schools to increase our nation's competitiveness in science and technology development. The term began to be used in education to address the perceived lack of qualified candidates for high-tech jobs. It has been used since the Sputnik era and revived fairly regularly since, and it captures the idea that maintaining a citizenry well versed in the STEM fields is a vital component of emphasis in the public education agenda of the United States.

We next give definitions of each of the four domains of STEM, as this book will focus on PBI enacted in the context of these four disciplines. We draw upon the definitions used in the National Research Council (NRC, 2014) report on STEM integration:

> Science is the study of the natural world, including the laws of nature associated with physics, chemistry, and biology and the treatment or application of facts, principles, concepts, or conventions associated with these disciplines. Science is both a body of knowledge that has been accumulated over time and a process—scientific inquiry—that generates new knowledge. Knowledge from science informs the engineering design process.

> Technology, while not a discipline in the strictest sense, comprises the entire system of people and organizations, knowledge, processes, and devices that go into creating and operating technological artifacts, as well as the artifacts themselves. Throughout history, humans have created technology to satisfy their wants and needs. Much of modern technology is a product of science and engineering, and technological tools are used in both fields.
>
> Engineering is both a body of knowledge—about the design and creation of human-made products—and a process for solving problems. This process is design under constraint. One constraint in engineering design is the laws of nature, or science. Other constraints include time, money, available materials, ergonomics, environmental regulations, manufacturability, and reparability. Engineering utilizes concepts in science and mathematics as well as technological tools.
>
> Mathematics is the study of patterns and relationships among quantities, numbers, and space. Unlike in science, where empirical evidence is sought to warrant or overthrow claims, claims in mathematics are warranted through logical arguments based on foundational assumptions. The logical arguments themselves are part of mathematics along with the claims. As in science, knowledge in mathematics continues to grow, but unlike in science, knowledge in mathematics is not overturned, unless the foundational assumptions are transformed. Specific conceptual categories of K–12 mathematics include numbers and arithmetic, algebra, functions, geometry, and statistics and probability. Mathematics is used in science, engineering, and technology. (p. 14)

The term STEM is also sometimes used to address the concern that the subjects are often taught in isolation, instead of as an integrated whole—an idea more formally referred to as "STEM integration." STEM integration advocates generally support expanding the study of engineering within each of the other subject areas (science, math, and technology) and beginning the study of engineering during the elementary school years. They also advocate for bringing STEM education to all students rather than only gifted programs. However, we know that high school success in STEM subjects is often determined many years earlier. By developing an interest in the natural and social sciences and in STEM in preschool or immediately following school entry, the possibility of STEM success in high school can be greatly improved. Research shows that school integration can also support the achievement of African American, Hispanic, and Native American students (Morgan et al., 2016). STEM integration is a natural habitat for PBI techniques, which offer important opportunities to use ideas from multiple disciplines simultaneously to solve complex problems.

The idea of STEM does come with some criticism (Teitelbaum, 2014). For instance, the focus on increasing participation in STEM fields has attracted some negative attention. Some have criticized the efforts of the

U.S government to increase the number of STEM graduates, saying that among studies on the subject, no one has been able to find evidence of widespread labor market shortages or hiring difficulties in science and engineering occupations that require bachelor's degrees or higher. In addition, they argue that some studies indicate that real wages in many—but not all—science and engineering occupations have been flat or slow growing, and unemployment is high or higher than in many comparably skilled occupations. Some have also suggested that science should not be grouped with the other three STEM categories because, whereas the other three generally result in high-paying jobs, the sciences, especially the life sciences, tend to pay below the overall median for recent college graduates. Additionally, some advocates seek for the inclusion of the arts into STEM and call for an approach emphasizing STEAM and others advocate for the inclusion of both the arts and reading into the STEM conversations as STREAM.

Now that we have a clear definition of what we mean by our context of "STEM education," we move to discussing the primary topic of this book: project-base instruction.

Defining PBI

PBI is a pedagogical approach where students learn key STEM principles through the extended investigation of driving questions or inquiries. In Project-based STEM classrooms, students investigate, utilize technological tools, construct artifacts, participate in debates, collaborate, and make products to demonstrate what they have learned. Informed by and in parallel to what scientists do, Project-based science embodies both the nature of inquiry and the nature of the scientific enterprise. PBI is a method informed by what is known about how children learn. It not only helps students learn STEM subject matter, it also enables them to learn STEM more thoroughly and deeply.

PBI is not rigidly defined and can be referred to by other names including project-based learning and case-based learning. This method incorporates a variety of instructional approaches, and differentiating between PBI and other methods is not always straightforward. However, PBI has specific elements including a driving question, a tangible product, an investigation, use of cognitive tools, collaboration, assessments and the opportunity for revision, and extensive scaffolding (Marshall et al., 2010). These elements make PBI a powerful method for teaching mathematics and science by giving students first-hand experience with what professionals do while also helping them retain and apply academic knowledge (Pellegrino & Brophy, 2008). Through a dynamic process of investigation and collaboration and using the same processes and technologies that real scientists, applied mathematicians, and engineers use, students in PBI classrooms work in teams to formulate questions, make predictions, design investigations, collect and analyze data, make products, and share ideas. Students learn fundamental science and mathematical principles that they apply to their daily lives, often using technology as part of their investigations.

PBI is designed to develop deep conceptual understanding and mastery of subject-area content while also making explicit the underlying connections between STEM disciplines. PBI develops proficiency in core mathematics and scientific practices, develops research and information analysis skills, and integrates considerations of content and pedagogy for teachers. Teachers in PBI settings must build strong connections between educational theory and practice; integrate themes of assessment, equity, literacy, and technology into their teaching; and cultivate reflective practice.

When considering the planning and structure of PBI, four common design principles of Project-based environments for teachers are emphasized: (a) defining learning appropriate goals that lead to deep understanding; (b) providing scaffolds such as using "embedded teaching," "teaching tools," and a set of "contrasting cases"; (c) including multiple opportunities for formative self-assessment; and (d) developing social structures that promote participation and revision. As further explained in Chapter 3, projects that meet these requirements can be referred to as a "Big P" Project, distinguished from a "little p" project. PBI is situated within learning environments and the goals these environments encompass—which brings in our next topic of national standards.

PBI and National Standards

In 2010, the National Governors Association Center for Best Practices (and the Council of Chief State School Officers) released the Common Core State Standards (CCSS) for Mathematics (CCSS Initiative, 2010). These standards include both overarching standards for mathematical practice, as well as standards specific to particular mathematical grade levels and domains (e.g., algebra). Forty-two states in the U.S. have adopted the CCSS.

In 2013, the NRC, the National Science Teachers Association, the American Association for the Advancement of Science, and Achieve developed the Next Generation Science Standards (NGSS). The NGSS are composed of three dimensions: overarching scientific and engineering practices; disciplinary core ideas specific to the domains of physical sciences, life sciences, earth and space science, and technology; and crosscutting concepts that have applications across scientific domains. Eighteen states in the U.S. have adopted these standards.

The current CCSS and NGSS reform initiatives place an increased emphasis on developing depth of discipline-specific content knowledge and conceptual understanding; building skills in fundamental science, mathematical, and engineering practices; and applying science and mathematics to solve authentic problems. This in turn necessitates the preparation of teachers with deep content knowledge who have experience designing, carrying out, analyzing, and presenting independent scientific inquiries; constructing and defending logic-based mathematical arguments; applying mathematical tools and practices to solve complex problems and model scientific phenomena; and designing Project-based learning environments for all learners.

The CCSS for mathematics insists upon rigor and emphasize problem-solving and mathematical thinking. There is also attention and focus on conceptual understanding and realistic or authentic contexts. Similarly, the NGSS demand for an approach to science instruction that more closely embodies the work of practicing scientists and engineers. The NGSS emphasize deep conceptual understanding of core ideas over breadth of content coverage and the integration of science knowledge with the practices needed to engage in scientific inquiry and engineering design.

Table 1.1 shows a detailed alignment of elements of PBI to the CCSS Mathematical Practices and the NGSS Scientific and Engineering Practices. As can be seen from Table 1.1, PBI is an effective approach for allowing students to meet the CCSS and NGSS. This is because PBI involves the investigation of complex, real-world problems; the collection and analysis of data; the creation of explanatory models and tangible products; the construction of explanations that show pattern and structure; the presentation of STEM principles and project findings to an audience; and the use of STEM discipline-specific technological tools.

Differentiating PBI From Other Approaches

PBI is often confused with other teaching methods, particularly instructional methods that are problem-based, case-based, challenge-based, and inquiry-based, as well as with cyclical instruction methods, such as the Learning Cycle and the Legacy Cycle. In the following section, we differentiate PBI from each of these approaches.

Table 1.1

Alignment of PBI Elements to CCSS and NGSS Practices for K–12 Classrooms

8 CCSS Mathematical Practices (MP)	8 NGSS Scientific and Engineering Practices	Elements of the practice of PBI
MP1: Make sense of problems and persevere in solving them	1. Asking questions (for science) and defining problems (for engineering)	Students use inquiry methods, with support from teachers, to pose and investigate questions and problems, in a problem-based and/or project-based setting.
MP2: Reason abstractly and quantitatively	2. Developing and using models	Students develop explanatory models based on core STEM principles to explain real-world phenomena and to drive the creation of tangible products.
MP3: Construct viable arguments and critique the reasoning of others	7. Engage in argument from evidence	Students must address the driving question by leveraging STEM principles and ideas, as well as data, and present their findings and ideas to audiences, both internal and external. Students must self-reflect and also give their peers critical feedback.
MP4: Model with mathematics	4. Analyzing and interpreting data	Students often accomplish project goals by integrating relevant technology into their project-based investigations (e.g., internet, simulations, data analysis packages, modeling software, etc.). Students may critically examine data to test hypotheses and develop arguments.
MP5: Use appropriate tools strategically	5. Using mathematics and computational thinking	Students may use a variety of computational tools (e.g., statistical software) and mathematical tools (e.g., rulers, balances) to carry out project-based investigations and gather and analyze data for these investigations.
	6. Planning and carrying out investigations	Students use inquiry methods to carefully plan and carry out project-based investigations to answer driving questions.
	8. Obtaining, evaluating, and communicating information	

(Table continued on next page)

Table 1.1 (Continued)

Alignment of PBI Elements to CCSS and NGSS Practices for K–12 Classrooms

8 CCSS Mathematical Practices (MP)	8 NGSS Scientific and Engineering Practices	Elements of the practice of PBI
MP6: Attend to precision MP7: Look for and make use of structure MP8: Look for and express regularity in repeated reasoning	3. Constructing explanations (for science) and designing solutions (for engineering)	Students make sense of the data they collect through a project investigation by constructing explanations or designs that answer the driving question, involve STEM principles, and represent key patterns or findings in the data they drew upon.

Problem-Based Learning

Problem-based learning and PBI share a number of similarities. Specifically, both methods:

- begin with a challenge or problem task presented to the students, which is based on real-world issues and contexts;
- are learner centered in that they involve the teacher as a facilitator and students working in groups;
- provide scaffolding to manage cognitive load and incorporate formative and summative assessments;
- involve higher thinking skills where students deal with concepts and principles; and
- have been found to be engaging and motivating to students.

Despite their similarities, problem-based learning and PBI differ in the following ways:

- There is little-to-no direct instruction in problem-based learning, but direct instruction is used in PBI, often in a "just-in-time" manner.
- In problem-based learning, students are solving a problem, whereas in PBI, students are developing or creating a product in

response to a driving question. This distinction can be likened to constructing solutions versus designing products.
- In problem-based learning, students' work is only "open-ended" with respect to the fact that there are many approaches that learners can use to get to a certain solution. In contrast, PBI has ill-defined complexity and open-endedness, but also has tangible outcomes that are tailored to the students' interests and abilities.

It is possible to use these two approaches strategically to supplement each other. Whereas problem-based learning often involves students collaboratively solving real-world problem investigations in multiple ways, PBI involves extended investigations of driving questions to create products or models. Problem-based scenarios can be presented and solved by students within individual lessons in a PBI unit. These problem-based lessons can be presented in a "just-in-time" manner, as students develop the need to learn central STEM concepts for their Project that the problem-based lesson will help them to explore and understand. Thus, a problem-based lesson can provide the basis for thinking about a PBI unit and thus serve as a scaffold. For example, a project about doing financial planning for a school carnival that students will host could begin with a problem-based scenario where students must price particular carnival games that are presented in the context of the carnival that has already been structured and planned by other students with full financial information available. Following a problem-based scenario with a Project can lead students to develop more flexible skills and understanding.

Case-Based Learning

Case-based learning also has similar elements to PBI (Williams, 1992). Both of these methods involve situated learning where students explore problems in real-world contexts. When we say that learning is *situated*, we mean that learning is most meaningful when it takes place in the context of an authentic problem situation—a situation that STEM practitioners might actually confront in doing their work. Situativity theory suggests that people learn new ideas by participating in communities of practice. This learning results from being part of real scientific discussions and investigations and participating in investigations in order to understand and contribute to what is happening. PBI has a background rooted in constructivist and situated learning theories (Krajcik & Blumenfeld, 2006), as does case-based learning.

Both case-based learning and PBI methods also provide scaffolding. Additionally, both involve the teacher being a facilitator and students working in groups or collaboration. Students are able to collect a wide range of information and data in pursuit of their goals (Herreid, 2007).

Case-based learning is popular in professional business and law schools. In case-based learning, students apply their knowledge to real-world scenarios, which are either imagined or have actually taken place. In case-based classrooms, students typically work in groups with cases involving one or more characters and/or scenarios. The cases present a disciplinary issue or problems for which students devise solutions under the guidance of the instructor and peers.

There are advantages to case-based learning including it provides students with a relevant opportunity to see theory in practice as authentic contexts which expose students to viewpoints from multiple sources and perspectives. Case-based learning also requires students to obtain and analyze data or information in order to reach a conclusion. Instructors who use case-based learning often indicate that their students are engaged, interested, and involved in the class. Finally, case-based learning develops analytic, communicative, and collaborative skills along with content knowledge. Students acquire substantive knowledge and develop analytic, collaborative, and communication skills (Wassermann, 1994).

There is a notable difference between case-based learning and PBI. Allchin (2013) noted different features and their related values and learning outcomes between case-based and problem-based learning and PBI, including the level of student autonomy; instructional focus on content, skills development, or nature-of-science understanding; the role of history, or known outcomes; scope, clarity, and authenticity of problems provided to students; extent of collaboration; complexity, in terms of number of interpretive perspectives; and, perhaps most importantly, the role of applying versus generating knowledge.

In case-based learning, students are presented with a story or a narrative with issues that need to be solved. Not only are students thinking, but they also are reading or acting out cases. Students are then able to play different roles. Case-based learning usually involves a class discussion that gives students an opportunity to explore, analyze, and debate. With the knowledge gained from these experiences, students can adapt solutions to solve new problems. Case-based learning involves developing the experiences from cases, whereas PBI has experiences to challenge the students, leading to a creation.

Challenge-Based Instruction

Challenge-based instruction was developed by Apple, Inc. in collaboration with various educators across the country. It launched in 2008 with a collaborative project called Apple Classrooms of Tomorrow-Today, whose purpose was to "identify the essential design principles of the 21st century learning environment" (Digital Promise, n.d.). Challenge-based instruction is intended to encourage students to use the technology they already use every day to solve-real world problems.

There are several similarities between challenge-based instruction and PBI. Challenge-based instruction starts with a big idea or concept that is important to K–12 students and to society such as violence, creativity, and peace. From those big ideas, essential questions are generated that "identify what is important to know about the big idea and refine and contextualize that idea" (Digital Promise, n.d.). This is very similar to the anchors presented to students in PBI in the form of videos that demonstrate a real-life situation that students relate to, so as to contextualize the project. Using the essential questions in challenge-based instruction, a challenge is presented to the students in which they are supposed to come up with a resulting product that can lead to or be a part of concrete, meaningful action (Digital Promise, n.d.). In PBI, the students are also presented with a challenge in the form of a driving question for which they have to find or create some kind of product to address. In challenge-based instruction, the students are expected to collaborate with each other, teachers, and experts both in their communities and across the world when they are working on their solution (Digital Promise, n.d.). This is similar to PBI, in that in PBI students must also collaborate with each other, teachers, and others in the community to create their final product. However, collaboration with experts from various places around the world is not explicitly expected for PBI as it is for challenge-based instruction.

In challenge-based instruction, the students are provided with guided questions, guided activities, and guided resources. Guided questions are similar to the formative assessment used in PBI; however, they are only generated by the students in order to help them in figuring out the challenge. Guided activities are similar to scaffolding activities that are used in PBI; they help the students get to the solution by providing more structure to the material that they are learning. Guiding resources support the activities and often take the form of experts, videos, websites, and databases (Digital Promise, n.d.). These resources are similar to those which students draw upon in PBI.

A variety of solutions are also expected with challenge-based instruction as well as PBI, as there is not just one correct solution. However, with challenge-based instruction, the solution must be presented in a multimedia format, such as videos and podcasts. Challenge-based instruction also has an assessment that comes after the solution is presented, which is similar to PBI's summative assessment expectation. An aspect of challenge-based instruction that is not explicitly included in PBI is that students must publish their challenge process online. This is so that they can contribute to the larger learning community (Digital Promise, n.d.). Challenge-based instruction might get confused with PBI in that they are similar in structure. However, this form of instruction is much more specific than PBI with respect to the process of the challenge and how the students are supposed to present their solution.

Inquiry-Based Learning

Inquiry-based learning is a type of instruction that involves students learning a concept through an investigation, sometimes in the form of a hands-on experiment. There are three different types of inquiry: structured, guided, and open. In structured inquiry, the teacher gives the students a problem with a set of procedures and materials and the students discover and interpret the outcome. In guided inquiry, the teacher provides the materials and the problem. It is up to the students to devise their own procedure. In open inquiry, which is more similiar to doing real science, the students come up with their own problem to investigate (Colburn, 2000).

Inquiry is very similar to PBI in that it involves student learning through asking questions. In inquiry-based learning, the teacher throughout the lesson asks the students questions. The students also ask questions and attempt to answer them throughout the inquiry. This is similar to PBI in that asking and answering questions is a form of formative self-assessment which is used in PBI.

Another similarity between inquiry-based learning and PBI is that students are usually exploring the material themselves. Students perform experiments and collect and analyze data in inquiry lessons. In Project-based lessons, they also carry out investigations and gather and interpret data. Students work collaboratively with each other, both in inquiry-based learning and PBI. In a typical inquiry lesson, there is an initial hook that captures the students' attention, usually in the form of a demonstration or the telling of a story. This is very similar to a driving question that is used in PBI.

While inquiry-based learning is very similar to PBI, PBI can be considered an extension of inquiry-based learning (Rivet & Krajcik, 2008). Inquiry-based learning can involve more teacher guidance than PBI, especially in the case of structured inquiry. With PBI, the teacher plays a role of overlooking students' progress as opposed to being directly involved. It was mentioned earlier that in both PBI and inquiry-based learning, students were asked questions and created their own questions that they then attempted to answer. In PBI, this is done in the form of formative and summative assessments at the end of the unit. In inquiry-based learning, this is done throughout the lesson.

An aspect of inquiry that might get confused with problem-based learning is that both involve a problem to be solved. In inquiry-based learning, the problem usually can be solved by one method, at least in structured inquiry. With problem-based learning, there can be more than one way to solve the problem, and the problem is usually based on a real-life situation. Problem-based learning is a more developed and structured form of inquiry-based learning, but inquiry-based learning is not an extension of problem-based learning (Rivet & Krajcik, 2008).

The Legacy Cycle

The Legacy Cycle (Schwartz et al., 1999) is an example of one way that PBI can be applied. There are many other possibilities for PBI's application, and the Legacy Cycle is not a complete or perfect embodiment of PBI. Thus, there are a number of characteristics of the Legacy Cycle that are comparable to characteristics of a generalized view of PBI, and there are likewise characteristics of the Legacy Cycle that do not strictly adhere to the basic tenets of PBI.

The Legacy Cycle shares a few defining attributes with PBI. Both methods, for instance, begin with a challenge and driving question that students follow and build off throughout the unit. Both methods provide copious amounts of scaffolding as students move through material, and both methods have opportunities for summative assessment at the end of their respective projects. The similarities between the two methods are all on the level of an overview, while the differences between the two as enumerated below are more concerned with details.

The differences between the Legacy Cycle and general forms of PBI mostly lie in the Legacy Cycle's inherent structure. The Legacy Cycle has a very specific structure that other forms of PBI do not necessarily need to follow. The Legacy Cycle usually involves much less direct instruction than PBI, as the Legacy Cycle relies on students researching and discovering information for themselves, while some forms of PBI allow for lectures and other methods of direct instruction from the classroom teachers. To this end, PBI's scaffolding usually comes in the form of worksheets or videos that add information to the students' knowledge base, while the Legacy Cycle's scaffolding tends to involve pointing out the students' knowledge gaps so that students can research and fill the gaps themselves rather than being told the next portion of information they need to know to complete the project. Because the Legacy Cycle is a type of PBI, it is easy to confuse the two. The Legacy Cycle embodies PBI, but PBI is not limited to application through the Legacy Cycle.

The Learning Cycle

The Learning Cycle is a project method modeled after Kolb's work in the area (http://changingminds.org/explanations/learning/kolb_learning.htm) and crafted to reflect principles of scientific inquiry. The Learning Cycle utilizes experiences that are "out of sync" with the students' intuition, which requires that they reflect on some phenomenon and attempt to use past experiences and understandings to explain it. When the students realize that their reflections cannot fully explain the topic being studied, they then form theories to reconcile their jarring experience with their knowledge of natural order to form new models that take the experience into account. In this manner, there is similarities to cognitive dissonance.[1] The students then put their theories to the test through experimentation and further reflection on the results of the experiments until they can explain the surprising phenomenon satisfactorily. The Learning Cycle can be essentially summed up as exploration, concept development, and concept application.

Like many of the other educational structures that PBI often gets confused with, the Learning Cycle shares several fundamental attributes with PBI. Both methods (a) begin with a challenge or problem that arouses student curiosity, (b) encourage students to explore that problem through various activities and/or experiments, and (c) leave room for assessment before students may move on to a new topic. Comparisons between PBI and the Learning Cycle indicate that differences, as with many other PBI-versus-other-methods comparisons, are in the details.

The Learning Cycle's general structure and execution showcase some fundamental differences. The Learning Cycle does not necessarily employ any overt scaffolding. In this approach, students are generally encouraged to discover on their own, rather than be systematically provided with information or with stepwise instructions. The Learning Cycle also can be easily instituted as either an individual activity or in a cooperative learning environment. Contrarily, PBI as a general rule is not universally conducive to implementation in both; most PBI projects lend themselves more easily to cooperative learning than to individual projects. Finally, the Learning Cycle and PBI differ majorly in that the Learning Cycle, like the Legacy Cycle, has little use or time for direct instruction, whereas PBI makes use of direct instruction whenever the occasion calls for it. The Learning Cycle relies on students' own innate curiosity to ensure that the students learn the material, whereas teachers utilizing PBI will present information to their students.

The Learning Cycle can be confused with PBI because of the shared pedagogy between the two methods. Both methods employ some type of driving question to encourage student participation and encourage some type of experimentation to enable students to discover the answer, or multiple answers, to the driving question. The confusion between the two methods is due to the fact that they share such similar pedagogy, but they have entirely different ways of executing that pedagogy.

SUMMARY

In this chapter, we gave an introduction to STEM and STEM integration in order to situate our discussion of PBI in this book. We then defined PBI, described its connection to national standards, and differentiated it from other approaches. These other varied methods of educational instruction are all often confused with PBI for a myriad of reasons, but it is possible to filter out the differences between each respective method and PBI. In the next chapter, we will discuss the history of PBI and its roots in the "project method," as well as why PBI is important and some critiques of PBI.

REFERENCES

Allchin, D. 2013. Problem- and case–based learning in science: An introduction to distinctions, values and outcomes. *CBE–Life Science Education, 12*(3), 364–372. https://doi.org/10.1187/cbe.12-11-0190

Colburn, A. (2000). An inquiry primer. *Science Scope, 23*(6), 42–44.

Common Core State Standards Initiative. (2010). *Mathematics glossary.* http://www.corestandards.org/the-standards/mathematics

Digital Promise. (n.d.). *Challenge-based learning.* http://digitalpromise.org/initiative/challenge-based-learning/

Festinger, L. (1957). *A theory of cognitive dissonance.* Stanford University Press.

Herreid, C. F. (2007). *Start with a story: The case study method of teaching college science.* NSTA Press.

Krajcik, J. S., & Blumenfeld, P. C. (2006). Project-based learning. In R. K. Sawyer (Ed.), *The Cambridge handbook of the learning sciences* (pp. 317–333). Cambridge University Press.

Marshall, J. A., Petrosino, A. J., & Martin, T. (2010). Preservice teachers' conceptions and enactments of project-based instruction. *Journal of Science Education and Technology, 19*(4), 370–386. https://doi.org//10.1007/s10956-010-9206-y

Morgan, P. L., Farkas, G., Hillemeier, M. M., & Maczuga, S. (2016). Science achievement gaps begin very early, persist, and are largely explained by modifiable factors. *Educational Researcher, 45*(1), 18–35. https://doi.org/10.3102/0013189X16633182

National Research Council. (2013). *Next Generation Science Standards: For states, by states*. National Academies Press.

National Research Council. (2014). *STEM integration in K-12 education: Status, prospects, and an agenda for research*. National Academies Press. https://doi.org/10.17226/18612

Pellegrino, J. W., & Brophy, S. (2008). From cognitive theory to instructional practice: Technology and the evolution of anchored instruction. In D. Ifenthaler, P. Pirnay-Dummer, & J. M. Spector (Eds.), *Understanding models for learning and instruction* (pp. 277–303). Springer.

Rivet, A. E., & Krajcik, J. S. (2008). Contextualizing instruction: Leveraging students' prior knowledge and experiences to foster understanding of middle school science. *Journal of Research in Science Teaching*, *45*(1), 79–100. https://doi.org/10.1002/tea.20203

Schwartz, D. L., X. Lin, Brophy, S., & Bransford, J. D. (1999). Toward the development of flexibly adaptive instructional designs. In C. M. Reigelut (Ed.), *Instructional design theories and models: Volume 11*. Erlbaum.

Teitelbaum, M. S. (2014, March). The myth of the science and engineering shortage. *The Atlantic*. https://www.theatlantic.com/education/archive/2014/03/the-myth-of-the-science-and-engineering-shortage/284359/

Wassermann, S. (1994). *Introduction to case method teaching: A guide to the galaxy*. Teachers College Press.

Williams, S. M. (1992). Putting case-based learning into context: Examples from legal, business, and medical education. *Journal of the Learning Sciences*, *2*(4), 367–427. https://doi.org/10.1207/s15327809jls0204_2

ENDNOTE

1. Learning processes involve the integration of new information into existing knowledge structures or schema. When new information is presented to learners that is unfamiliar or contradictory to their existing knowledge or schema, this triggers a phenomenon referred to as cognitive dissonance (Festinger, 1957).

CHAPTER 2

LINKING THE HISTORY OF THE "PROJECT METHOD" TO CURRENT PBI MOVEMENTS

THE PROJECT METHOD

In the last 10–15 years, the educational realm has directed a great deal of attention towards PBI. Many educators believe this phenomenon is a recent development in response to society's desire to enhance problem-solving abilities and create a passion for learning in the 21st century student. However, PBI closely resembles an educational movement in the 1920s known as the project method. The project method evolved as an alternative to the social efficiency movement, which based its curriculum in the "minimum essentials … set out to be learned" (Kliebard, 2004, p. 140). William Heard Kilpatrick, the father of the project method, proposed a philosophy in which learning facts that could be used later in life was secondary to learning as a part of life. As educators looked for ways to implement Kilpatrick's philosophy into subject matter, it grew into a curriculum. Even though the project method and PBI are separated by approximately 70 years, these two educational ideas are surprisingly more similar than different.

In the following sections, we explore how the following elements in the project method compare to PBI: (a) how a "project" is defined; (b) the objectives of the instruction; (c) how the curriculum is planned by teachers; (d) the time requirements of implementation; (e) connections to content students need to learn; (f) students' development of content knowledge, problem-solving skills, and transferrable knowledge; (g) the requirements for implementation; (h) the role of the school; (i) the attitudes of students, teachers, parents, and the community; (j) the alternatives to full implementation; (k) the resources required; and (l) the role of assessment.

Defining Project

Despite the fact that both methods begin with the word "project," interpreting project as the completion of a stereotypical student project is an oversimplification. The purpose of a project in these methods is to create a framework for student choice and engagement. Kilpatrick et al. (1921) said "no curriculum or technique will ever permit cut and dried projects because letting it be child oriented is an original and necessary factor" (p. 292). Kilpatrick (1925) proposed four different types of projects to meet a variety of student needs. The first type was to create or build, the second to simply enjoy, the third to solve a problem, and the fourth to learn specific knowledge.

The intent of PBI as we define it today coincides with this method. In order for a project to qualify as such, it must have a driving question which has multiple possible solutions (Bender, 2012). The open-endedness of the project-based method enables students to be innovative in creating a tangible product. Even though both methods recognize the importance of appropriate execution of projects, the initiative determining the directionality of the project varies slightly.

Determining Objectives

The most crucial characteristic of the project method is the incorporation of purpose within the activity. The project is most effectively implemented when the student is the driving force behind the inquiry (Hotchkiss, 1924). For instance, a student might come into class and ask why the leaves on the trees change colors in the fall. This is the determining purpose that initiates the project method process. The teacher's role then becomes creating a classroom experience that allows children to come to a conclusion on their own while increasing their knowledge. Therefore, the teacher is constructing activities in which learning subject content occurs through completing the task at hand.

The project method is constructed around the idea of "purposeful activities" (Kilpatrick, 1925, p. 348), whereas the focus in PBI, as conceptualized here, is on a driving question. The driving question, usually content related, is often developed by the teacher and planned in advance but may also be generated by student groups. Once the driving question has been developed, the teacher then creates opportunities for the students to have choice within the project. So instead of student interest determining the topic of study in the project method, the topic is often predetermined by the teacher in PBI, and the driving question is used to focus the project while student choice increases student interest.

Curriculum Planning

In the project method, the teacher has little control over the content that is studied, often is still responsible for the development of the activities and curriculum to help the student gain knowledge. The project method creates a complex situation for the teacher "if he plans too well, he will miss the mark; and if he does not plan at all, he will accomplish nothing" (Hotchkiss, 1924, pp. 43–44). Even though the project method is loosely structured (Hosic & Chase, 1924), a general guide was developed to aid the teacher in creating meaningful projects. The guide stressed that the process should always begin with a driving question that comes from a personal or social experience of the student. Once the purpose is established, the teacher should clarify the project; create ultimate and immediate aims; determine materials; create procedure; allow the students to explore; and, upon completion, provide time for reflection (Hotchkiss, 1924).

In PBI implemented today, as conceptualized in this book, the teacher establishes the order of subject matter, but the Project has built-in options to increase student engagement through ownership and choice. Instructional steps to create PBI units are readily available through a variety of resources for teachers to utilize. Even though there are multiple variations of the process, most approaches to PBI generally encompass a sequence of instructional steps that include: (a) introducing an idea; (b) developing a driving question; (c) creating opportunities for inquiry, innovation, investigation; and (d) presenting a product (Bender, 2012). Student choice should be encouraged throughout the process to increase intrinsic interest.

Time Requirements

A major issue determined by both teachers in the 1920s and current teachers is the amount of time required to employ a curriculum that uses projects. Even with a variety of resources helping teachers with implementation, there can still be apprehension due to time requirements and content coverage. The project method recognizes the amount of planning done by the teacher but suggests sharing the planning with the students in order to alleviate this time requirement. Once the project begins, "the teacher was required to do but little except act as chairman of the meeting and enable the group to carry on its work without confusion or waste of time" (Hosic & Chase, 1924, pp. 39–40).

A similar issue exists today when considering the use of PBI. A study of preservice teachers showed that the most common barrier to implementing PBI was inadequate time (Marshall et al., 2010). It is important to note, however, that although the workload is heavy in the beginning, the work decreases over the course of the project as the teacher becomes more of a guide. The additional resources discovered by students, the issues revealed, and the adjustments that are made can all be used to help the teacher modify the project for upcoming years. These will also help the teacher modify future projects and should eventually alleviate apprehension of time requirements for implementation.

Content Inclusion

Another area of concern for both the project method and PBI is inclusion of subject content. Some of the biggest opponents to the project method believed that having student-driven purposeful projects was mutually exclusive to covering content. Having students choose the topic of study can be problematic if these two areas are not aligned (Kilpatrick et al., 1921). Activities that have the greatest interest to children may not have high educational value. Frederick Bonser, an advocate for the project method, made the following argument:

> The project method raises no opposition between the appropriate interest and activities of children and the desirable subject matter out of which the courses of study should be made. It rather emphasizes bringing the two together in a manner that makes the worth and importance of the subject matter clearly apparent through the purpose. (as cited in Kilpatrick et al., 1921, p. 303)

Since the current system of education demands that teachers follow standards for content coverage (Mitchell et al., 2009), it is again a concern that not all content can be covered when implementing PBI. In a conventional classroom, it is much easier to gauge the amount of content delivered because it is happening in a traditionally sequential manner. PBI requires a teacher to be cognizant of the standards being implemented in each Project so that the end result has all content standards covered. However, both the project method and PBI stress the important difference between content coverage and content understanding.

Content Understanding

An argument in support of the project method and PBI is that it increases students' understanding of academic content. Project method supporters believe that the development of a purpose will ensure deeper and more meaningful learning of the content. It is thought that "the stronger the purpose the greater the tendency to push ahead in the face of obstacles and, accordingly, the greater the likelihood of success" (Kilpatrick, 1925, p. 202). A 4-year study from 1917–1921 comparing two schools, a control school with a traditional curriculum approach and an experimental school adopting the project method, was conducted to compare student achievement. The results showed that across grades it would take the control school a 0.382 fractional part of a school year longer to accomplish the same attainment as the experimental school (Collings, 1923). These results originally demonstrated the effect of student-derived purpose in developing understanding of content in an educational setting. Since then, there have been many studies indicating the benefits and attributes of PBI (see Krajcik & Shin, 2014, for a comprehensive review).

The rationale underlying PBI is that students will achieve more because they are more engaged and invested in learning the content (Bender, 2012). By framing content in the form of a project, a student can "create meaning from the chaos of a plethora of information" (Bender, 2012, p. 22). In a more recent study, Project-based economics classes were compared to control textbook/lecture economics classes (Finkelstein et al., 2010). The PBI classes scored better than the control group in both content knowledge and problem-solving skills on a standardized test of economic literacy. This demonstrates that PBI not only increases content understanding but also improves a student's ability to solve problems.

Problem-Solving Skills

An underlying idea in all of the original project method literature is the use of purpose-driven projects to enhance problem-solving skills. Beyond students learning content, the project method was teaching students how to think for themselves. If "one learns to do a thing by doing that thing; one doesn't learn to do his own thinking, therefore, by letting another do it for him" (Hosic & Chase, 1924, pp. 12–13). Proponents of the project method saw value in the student being able to recognize a problem and create a method for solving it. An argument against the project method's motivation for teaching problem-solving is that if a student is so focused on solving a problem, then their research would be limited to only what was necessary. Consequently, a serious limit is placed on the breadth of learning if the only valuable knowledge is the knowledge needed to solve a specific problem (Kilpatrick et al., 1921).

In today's society where knowledge bases in subject areas are rapidly changing (Bender, 2012), problem-solving skills are considered a necessity for keeping pace with the world in which we live. PBI is a way of teaching that focuses on problem-solving skills and higher levels of induction than traditional forms of classroom instruction. The problems faced in a PBI unit should be authentic and centered in real-world application to allow for these skills to transfer to the problems faced in life.

Transferring Knowledge and Skills

The project method and PBI allow for both knowledge and skills to be learned through application. This allows ideas to be grounded within a framework as opposed to abstract ideas that need to be memorized. The project method claims that learning within this structure allows the skills to be transferred to other applications. Bagley believed this claim of "transfer potency" (as cited in Kilpatrick et al., 1921, p. 289) to be only an assumption of the project method, as it had yet to be experimentally tested. Bagley argued that in fact, "there is some indirect evidence that information gained primarily to solve an immediate problem is *not* so long retained nor so easily recalled as is information that is mastered with the intent to make its mastery permanent" (Kilpatrick et al., 1921, pp. 288–290). Bagley did not intend for the project method to be abandoned completely but only refined to include various forms of instruction including direct teaching. Since the time of project method, research has been carried out to determine the validity of the claim that PBI enhances knowledge transfer. It is said that "transfer is most likely to … occur in an environment that is characterized by meaningful activity, expert guidance, and knowledge-building collaboration" (Howard, 2002, p. 347). These characteristics are the backbone of PBI.

Other research studying the connection between PBI and knowledge transfer has determined that transfer occurs when the relationship between information and knowledge is understood (Lou et al., 2011). PBI provided the basis for such a symbiosis (Mitchell et al., 2009). Content understanding, development of problem-solving skills, and successful knowledge transfer are very strong arguments in favor of school implementation of either curriculum.

Requirements of Full Implementation

The intent of the project method approach was to be adopted wholeheartedly by a school system because it transcends grade level and subject matter. In order for a project to include a variety of content, "a radical change must be made in the old traditional curricula; a new organization must provide larger units of worth-while subject matter" (Hotchkiss, 1924,

p. 43). The project method experimental school that was previously mentioned restructured grade levels into three different age groups of students, 4- to 6-year-olds, 7- to 9-year-olds, and 10- to 14-year-olds. It also divided the school day by types of projects such as story, hand, play, and excursion, as opposed to subject matter. These classifications of projects were not the original types proposed by Kilpatrick. However, they were specifically developed to meet the needs of a functioning school while creating purposeful activities the students could naturally engage in.

Presently, a variety of schools have established their structure around PBI. The New Tech Network provides support to schools attempting to implement PBI. According to New Tech Network (n.d.), learning should be "contextual, creative, and shared." This is accomplished by integrating subject matter and employment of technology. Even though the New Tech Network and various other programs have adopted PBI as their curriculum, it is still being applied within a preestablished framework. Many supporters of full implementation of PBI embrace a new culture of schooling (Solomon, 2003), which eliminates the confines of the modern school system such as specific subject classes, class time limitations, and universally applied graduation requirements.

School Perspective

The management of school resources is a concern that transcends time in the field of education. Many thought the project method was wasteful when compared to the curriculum of social efficiency theory, which states that schools should run like a factory that maximize product while minimizing time and resources. The project method was considered inefficient, as it was grounded in student-driven projects that allow a student to learn at their own unique pace with numerous resources. However, James Fleming Hosic opposed this view by saying,

> The project method is economical. If true measures are applied to the results, it will be found that more and better learning takes place in a given period when work is going in the spirit of the project method than otherwise. (as cited in Kilpatrick et al., 1921, pp. 305–306)

In other words, if content understanding is increased using the project method, then the amount of time and resources is considered an investment in a student's future. Another concern was class size and the belief that one teacher cannot successfully accommodate the needs of so many students doing projects while still obtaining successful learning results (Kilpatrick et al., 1921).

There are also concerns of the wastefulness in current PBI. One issue of implementation is the "cost of changing the curriculum and then maintaining the new program" (Azer, 2001, p. 391). By changing from a traditional classroom to a Project-based classroom, a school would need to invest in different resources and make technology readily available to the students. PBI is based in real-world, present-day Projects, so the resources and technology need to be updated continually to keep the assignments current.

PBI also requires a smaller class size. Therefore, additional instructors with "flexible classroom space" would be needed for implementation. However, addressing the concerns of the school is only part of the resistance to full implementation (see Wright et al., 2019, for an informed discussion on class size and learning).

Attitude of Students

With both the project method and PBI focused on student engagement, it can be assumed that the way in which students view education might change drastically. Hotchkiss (1924) believed that a student's acceptance of learning through the project method would increase over time. Therefore, any initial hesitation by the child would eventually diminish with continued exposure to this method of education. When H. R. Hatch, a history teacher using the project method, asked his ninth- and 10th-grade students what they felt were the good features of the project method, they answered that they were motivated to work harder because of the choice that the project method involved (Kilpatrick et al., 1921). The project method implemented in the experimental school showed a positive change in the view students had about school. School enrollment increased only 4% in the control school and 25% in the experimental school. There was also a major increase in the number of students attending school every day, a decrease in the number of tardies and truancies, and an increase in the number of students graduating eighth grade and continuing their scholastic studies (Collings, 1923).

PBI experiences a wider range of implementation issues pertaining to students' attitude than the project method. The typical school system has the teacher as a dispenser of knowledge and facts for students to learn. In order for PBI to be effective, a student has to understand there is the possibility of no or multiple correct answers to a problem and that mistakes will be made throughout the process. Another difficulty exists in the students' attitude towards the Project-based units themselves. A Project must be engaging in order for students to invest the significant amount of effort this work entails. Along the same lines, a Project that is too difficult can cause frustration and make it difficult for students to want to deeply engage in Project work (Blumenfeld et al., 1991). Therefore, a balance between educationally rich projects and student interests must exist in every project. Determining that balance is the responsibility of the teacher, and it is one of many difficulties the teacher faces.

Attitudes of Teachers

The ability of the teacher to use the students' interests to create meaningful projects is the most important aspect of the project method. Teacher's beliefs about PBI are critical to the success of the project method. The experimental school recognized this fact when implementing their project curriculum, so a major focus was on the teachers' attitudes during the process. They also had 120 teachers come to observe how the project method was implemented. When surveyed, only one of the 120 teachers expressed a desire to remain teaching at the traditional school (Collings, 1923). This enthusiasm could be due in part to the re-invigorating the role a teacher fulfills in a classroom. The project method requires "teachers ... to keep themselves alive to the problems and interests of the time" but also inspires them to "stay young in spirit" (Kilpatrick et al., 1921, p. 304). In order to gain support for a curriculum, Tyler (1949) believed that evaluation of its impact needed to be communicated to parents and the public.

PBI, as conceptualized here, must be supported by teachers if it is to be adopted in classrooms. Professional development must be available for teachers to learn the process of PBI, and there also needs to be adequate support from the school. Administrators should understand that with so many variables, not every Project will work seamlessly every time. Teachers must be provided time for reflection and revision of Projects. Teachers must also be willing to adopt a new teaching philosophy, where they encourage students to be in charge of their own learning. Thus, attempting to implement PBI in a traditional school can be challenging, as significant teaching changes may be necessary (Solomon, 2003). Another obstacle in PBI is determining how the teacher assesses knowledge. The teacher must be able to communicate the successes of PBI.

Attitudes of Parents and Community

The project method was considered quite revolutionary compared to the social efficiency movement that was already in place. Parents were concerned that students were not getting the content knowledge they needed to be successful in later life. According to Collings (1923), "This conflict constituted one of the most serious factors that ... had to be overcome, since it involved a change of a deep-seated attitude toward the nature of school" (p. 17). As the project method was implemented in the experimental school, parent involvement was used to gauge the parents' attitude towards the new curriculum. In all facets that parent involvement was measured, there was an increase compared to the control school (Collings, 1923). The project method had "parents reporting that they were re-enjoying" learning alongside their children (Hosic & Chase, 1924, p. 109).

When schools today are implementing PBI, parent and community support is vital. Some of the PBI schools in the New Tech Network offer workshops for parents to enhance their understanding of the process, as well as to show them how to support their child's learning at home (New Tech Network, n.d.). The New Tech Network was created as a nonprofit organization to directly support other schools. As the network of schools grew, New Tech Network has evolved to provide support for a myriad of implementations and every demographic and community type.

This support helps develop a relationship between the parent, child, and school, which is critical given that relevant, real-world projects often involve communities and require resources within those communities (New Tech Network, n.d.). Through the students' attempt to solve community issues, an automatic connection is created between the students and the community in which they reside. These connections often help parents and communities develop a positive view of PBI, which is essential for full implementation of PBI.

Alternatives to Full Implementation

Schools adopting the project method or PBI must break away from the already established educational framework. Even though the project method was intended for full implementation throughout a school, Kilpatrick (1925) recognized this limitation and pleaded to "encourage thinking in your pupils. There is always some chance to think. Be on the lookout for problems lying with the course of study. Use such for all they are worth" (p. 354). Kilpatrick believed that the project method could positively affect students' learning even on a small scale. However, only fully adopting the educational philosophy in its purest form brings about the intended results of the project method.

The study of the preservice teachers previously discussed also showed that dealing with a prespecified curriculum (Marshall et al., 2010) was a major obstacle to implementing PBI. Bender (2012) suggested that to combat this issue in the current classroom, PBI should be introduced as an add-on to existing instructional units and then slowly adopted as a teacher becomes more comfortable with the process. Even with the intent being eventual full implementation, "to date, efforts at project-based pedagogy have primarily explored a 'replacement unit' approach, in which units are integrated into teacher's ongoing curricula" (Krajcik et al., 2008, p. 4). Advocates of both the project method and PBI believed that even if implementation on a large scale was not possible, the benefits of introducing purposeful projects into the curriculum would be considerable.

Additional Resources

The project method was founded with the intention of creating an environment of self-discovery. The experimental school redirected funds from the purchase of charts, posters, and textbooks towards resources that would allow students to uncover knowledge on their own—such as newspapers, library books, musical equipment, and science equipment. The study tracked what students chose to engage in at school, as well as how it affected them outside in their home life. The results demonstrate that a desire to learn and investigate in school transferred to the students' lives outside school (Collings, 1923). These results can be attributed to the student growing as a learner and developing a healthy desire to discover the world in which they live. Even without a variety of resources, "if the purpose is real to the children, they will find materials; they will manage with very little equipment" (Hosic & Chase, 1924, p. 100).

Today's technological society has almost endless resources for a student to investigate and learn. These technologies combine seamlessly into PBI. "Modern technology ... should be used in school to make the curriculum much more fun and relevant" (Bender, 2012, p. 79). The internet can be used for research, helping students to gather information relevant to the driving question. A variety of communication technologies can be used to encourage communication between students, teachers, and experts. Technology can also be used to create content and publish results. The "conjoining of project-based learning and technology has greatly increased learning opportunities" (Bender, 2012, p. 120) for a modern-day student. Because facts are so readily available, the need to memorize has diminished and the importance of a student's ability to process information and problem solve has increased. PBI coupled with technology has created a framework to develop these skills in students.

Assessment

Assessing and assigning grades was not a major part of the project method mentality. Kilpatrick (1925) addressed the school system that mandates assigning grades by saying, "Try to manage these marks so that they will do as little harm as possible" (p. 353). It was thought that the teacher should "judge ... not merely by the stated modicum of knowledge" but on a student's "mastery of the method of organization" (Hosic & Chase, 1924, pp. 69–70). A student being taught using the project method had no definite objectives in which learning could be measured against; instead, it was the purpose of the teacher to create a meaningful environment in which learning could occur.

PBI usually culminates with a final product to be evaluated by the teacher. There is in essence an unlimited number of ways a student could demonstrate their learning. This diversity of products requires a teacher to use a variety of evaluation techniques. Bender (2012) suggested that rubrics, self-evaluations, peer evaluations, and even portfolios could be used to gauge a student's learning. More important than how a teacher evaluates is how PBI allows evaluation to become part of the design process. "The key point here is that the curriculum materials and assessments are designed together in an iterative process" (Krajcik et al., 2008, p. 9) instead of traditional grading practices, where grading "represented everything but a celebration of student work" (Bender, 2012, p. 177). PBI that involves authentic, real-world problems with multiple answers allows a student to develop satisfaction in developing a product as well as mastery of a content area, and such assessments should address both the student activity as well as content knowledge acquisition.

The project method of the 1920s lost support from educators when the Great Depression created despondency with capitalism. The sense that a privileged few were deciding the outcome of many brought "a critical examination of American schools" (Kliebard, 2004, 154). The idea of social reconstruction became the new movement in educational curriculum. Even Kilpatrick was "drawn wholeheartedly into the new orbit" (Kliebard, 2004, p. 157). The ideals of the project method were discarded for creating schools with the intent of making socially aware citizens. A comparison between the two methods gives insight to the potential benefits, issues, and ultimate direction of PBI. Technology has played a major part in reinvigorated student-centered project-based approaches and could possibly be the factor that perpetuates these approaches into the future of education.

WHY PBI IS IMPORTANT

Research has indicated that PBI in science, math, and engineering has positive effects on student learning, gives students a deeper understanding of the content, and increases positive feelings towards the subject (Boaler, 1998; Cognition and Technology Group at Vanderbilt, 1997). For example, Petrosino et al. (2003) noted "impressive" student performance on both written and interview tasks relating to variation. Students in the PBI group outperformed fourth-grade students on the National Assessment of Educational Progress on two items that involved interpreting graphs, and they performed comparably to seventh and eighth graders in statistical reasoning (Petrosino et al., 2003). Moreover, Barron et al. (1998) examined the *Jasper Challenge Series* and found an increase in student performance on an assessment of business planning, mathematical concepts, and problem-solving.

There have been several meta-analyses that examined parts of PBI. Schroeder et al. (2007) performed a meta-analysis on the effects of different teaching strategies on science achievement for students in the United States. Sixty-one studies were analyzed, and Schroeder et al. found inquiry-based learning strategies had a positive effect size of .65 and collaborative learning strategies had an effect size of .95 on science achievement. Additionally, Springer et al. (1999) examined 39 studies for a meta-analysis on small group learning for undergraduates in STEM. They found that small-group learning increased positive attitudes toward learning (effect size of .51), increased academic achievement (effect size of .40), and increased persistence in the STEM courses (effect size of .46). Springer et al. found small-group learning led to a more positive attitude for women compared to men. Further, Furtak et al. (2012) performed an analysis of 37 experimental and quasi-experimental studies on inquiry-based learning in science. They found an overall effect size of .50 for inquiry-based learning. Despite the findings for inquiry-based learning in science and different teaching strategies, there is no meta-analysis on PBI in the STEM fields.

Some Critiques of PBI

Three criticisms or concerns have been raised about PBI: (a) insufficient structure or guidance provided to learners, (b) extent to which PBI is effective across subject matters, and (c) time constraints. The first criticism centers on a comparison between a more traditional instructional method that is structured and directive and others that are unstructured and student-driven. In one well-known critique of several instructional approaches that have some similarities to PBI, Kirschner et al. (2006) compared two types of learning. In one type, direct instruction, there is a learner and an instructor who tells the learner what to know. In this process of "learning," the instructor passes on information, teaches the process, and explains concepts fully so that a learner can move information from long-term memory to working memory. They defined the other type of learning as one where a learner is put into a minimally guided environment and expected to learn important information on their own. In minimally guided instruction, Kirschner et al. included problem-based learning, inquiry-based learning, experimental learning, and constructivist learning. They stated that minimally guided instruction is not as effective as direct instruction because of how it taxes working memory while not building knowledge in long-term memory, and they cited at least 10 different experiments that provided support for this conclusion. Kirschner et al. also mention that in an experiment conducted by Brown and Campione (1994), students receiving minimally guided instruction tended to get frustrated and confused, while they also had more misconceptions. In another experiment, Klahr and Nigam (2004) compared the quality of learning between guided instruction versus minimally guided instruction and found nothing conclusive. Building on these studies, Kirschner et al. concluded by arguing that the prevalence of minimally guided instruction is based upon peoples' ideologies, rather than supported by theory-based research findings.

As a reply to the Kirschner et al. (2006) point of view, Hmelo-Silver et al. (2007) argued that problem-based learning and inquiry-based learning do not fall under the category of minimally guided instruction. Instead, these approaches provide students with extensive scaffolding and guidance to facilitate student learning. Forms of scaffolding include direct instruction, expert information and guidance, and questions that promote student learning by modeling, coaching, and eventually fading some of their support. Teachers play a significant role in scaffolding learners' content knowledge on a just-in-time basis, as well as provide opportunities for students' mindful and productive engagement with the task and tools. The same could be said of PBI.

In addition, Hmelo-Silver et al. (2007) argued that although Kirshner et al. (2006) cited several studies and meta-analyses of problem-based learning that claimed the approaches were ineffective, they overlooked other reviews that showed a moderate effect size favoring problem-based learning (e.g., Dochy et al., 2003; Vernon & Blake, 1993). Also, results in some of the research cited by Kirshner et al. were inconclusive. The mixed effects of problem-based learning made the Kirshner et al. "evidence" of the ineffectiveness of problem-based learning inconclusive. In contrast, studies that showed significant and marked effect sizes and gains in favor of inquiry-based learning and problem-based learning have provided evidence for the effectiveness of these approaches (Geier et al., 2008; Hickey et al., 1999; Hickey et al., 2000; Lynch et al., 2005).

A second criticism of PBI specifically relates to its place in teaching, namely, the extent to which its effectiveness is the same throughout all subject areas. According to Beckett (2002), teachers and students tend to have a positive view of PBI and believe PBI allows for a richer experience in acquiring and retaining knowledge. Although PBI fares well with most subject areas, problems seem to arise when applying PBI in second language education.

Finally, time is a major issue for PBI. Teachers can either be successful in implementing PBI or fail to reach their goals. The amount of time that teachers spend on making a lesson plan and the time it takes the student to complete the project could be overwhelming (Colley, 2008). District standards can affect PBI dramatically; if not enough time is allowed for certain subjects and topics to be covered, PBI cannot thrive.

SUMMARY

The limitations of implementing the project method and PBI are similar. Both face challenges from a multitude of sources including schools, teachers, students, and parents or communities. PBI is a potentially powerful method to improve student attitudes and learning—it has a long history in schooling and many stories of success. However, it is not without controversy or logistical difficulty. The purpose of the remainder of this book is to walk STEM educators through the complex process of designing and implementing a Project-based unit. We seek to provide the tools relating to PBI knowledge that such teachers would need to be successful, while also continuing critical discussion about both the challenges and opportunities of PBI.

REFERENCES

Azer, S. A. (2001). Problem-based learning: Challenges, barriers and outcome issues. *Saudi Medical Journal, 22*(5), 389–397.

Barron, B. J., Schwartz, D. L., Vye, N. J., Moore, A., Petrosino, A., Zech, L., & Bransford, J. D. (1998). Doing with understanding: Lessons from research on problem-and project-based learning. *Journal of the Learning Sciences, 7*(3–4), 271–311.

Beckett, G. (2002). Teacher and student evaluations of project-based instruction. *TESL Canada Journal, 19*(2), 52–66.

Bender, W. N. (2012). *Project-based learning: Differentiating instruction for the 21st century*. Corwin Press.

Blumenfeld, P. C., Soloway, E., Marx, R. W., Krajcik, J. S., Guzdial, M., & Palincsar, A. (1991). Motivating project-based learning: Sustaining the doing, supporting the learning. *Educational Psychologist, 26*(3–4), 369–398.

Boaler, J. (1998). Open and closed mathematics: Student experiences and understandings. *Journal for Research in Mathematics Education, 29*(1), 41–62. https://doi.org/10.2307/749717

Brown, A. L., & Campione, J. C. (1994). Guided discovery in a community of learners. In K. McGilly (Ed.), *Classroom lesson: Integrating theory and classroom practice* (pp. 229–270). MIT Press.

Cognition and Technology Group at Vanderbilt. (1997). *The Jasper project: Lessons in curriculum, instruction, assessment, and professional development*. Erlbaum.

Colley, K. (2008). Project-based science instruction: A primer. *The Science Teacher, 75*(8), 23–28.

Collings, E. (1923). *An experiment with a project curriculum*. Macmillan.

Dochy, F., Segers, M., Van den Bossche, P., & Gijbels, D. (2003). Effects of problem-based learning: A meta-analysis. *Learning and Instruction, 13*(5), 533–568.

Finkelstein, N., Hanson, T., Huang, C. W., Hirschman, B., & Huang, M. (2010). *Effects of problem based economics on high school economics instruction* (NCEE 2010-4002). U.S. Department of Education, Institute of Education Sciences, National Center for Education Evaluation and Regional Assistance, Regional Educational Laboratory West.

Furtak, E. M., Seidel, T., Iverson, H., & Briggs, D. C. (2012). Experimental and quasi-experimental studies of inquiry-based science teaching: A meta-analysis. *Review of Educational Research, 82*(3), 300–329.

Geier, R., Blumenfeld, P. C., Marx, R. W., Krajcik, J. S., Fishman, B., Soloway, E., & Clay-Chambers, J. (2008). Standardized test outcomes for students engaged in inquiry-based science curricula in the context of urban reform. *Journal of Research in Science Teaching, 45*(8), 922–939.

Hickey, D. T., Kindfteld, A. C., Horwitz, P., & Christie, M. A. (1999). Advancing educational theory by enhancing practice in a technology-supported genetics learning environment. *Journal of Education, 181*(2), 25-55.

Hickey, D. T., Wolfe, E. W., & Kindfield, A. C. (2000). Assessing learning in a technology-supported genetics environment: Evidential and systemic validity issues. *Educational Assessment, 6*(3), 155–196.

Hmelo-Silver, C. E., Duncan, R. G., & Chinn, C. A. (2007). Scaffolding and achievement in problem-based and inquiry learning: A response to Kirschner, Sweller, and Clark (2006). *Educational Psychologist, 42*(2), 99–107.

Hosic, J. F., & Chase, S. E. (1924). *Brief guide to the project method*. World Book Company.

Hotchkiss, E. A. (1924). *The project method in classroom work*. Ginn & Company.

Howard, J. (2002). Technology-enhanced project-based learning in teacher education: Addressing the goals of transfer. *Journal of Technology and Teacher Education, 10*(3), 343–364.

Kilpatrick, W. H. (1925). *Foundations of method*. Macmillan.

Kilpatrick, W. H., Bagley, W. C., Bonser, F. G., Hosic, J. F., & Hatch, R. W. (1921, September). Dangers and difficulties of the project method and how to overcome them. *Teachers College Record, 22*, 283–321.

Kirschner, P. A., Sweller, J., & Clark, R. E. (2006). Why minimal guidance during instruction does not work: An analysis of the failure of constructivist, discovery, problem-based, experiential, and inquiry-based teaching. *Educational Psychologist, 41*(2), 75–86.

Klahr, D., & Nigam, M. (2004). The equivalence of learning paths in early science instruction: Effects of direct instruction and discovery learning. *Psychological Science, 15*(10), 661–667.

Kliebard, H. M. (2004). *The struggle for the American curriculum, 1893–1958*. Psychology Press.

Krajcik, J., McNeill, K. L., & Reiser, B. J. (2008). Learning-goals-driven design model: Developing curriculum materials that align with national standards and incorporate project-based pedagogy. *Science Education, 92*(1), 1–32.

Krajcik, J., & Shin, N. (2014). Project-based learning. In R. Sawyer (Ed.), *The Cambridge handbook of the learning sciences* (pp. 275–297). Cambridge University Press.

Lou, S., Shih, R., Ray Diez, C., & Tseng, K.-H. (2011). The impact of problem-based learning strategies on STEM knowledge integration and attitudes: An exploratory study among female Taiwanese senior high school students. *International Journal of Technology and Design Education, 21*, 195–215.

Lynch, S., Kuipers, J., Pyke, C., & Szesze, M. (2005). Examining the effects of a highly rated science curriculum unit on diverse students: Results from a planning grant. *Journal of Research in Science Teaching, 42*(8), 912–946.

Marshall, J., Petrosino, A., & Martin, T. (2010). Preservice teachers' conceptions and enactments of project-based instruction. *Journal of Science Education and Technology, 19*(4), 370–86.

Mitchell, S., Foulger, T. S., Wetzel, K., & Rathkey, C. (2009). The negotiated project approach: Project-based learning without leaving the standards behind. *Early Childhood Education Journal, 36*(4), 339–346.

New Tech Network. (n.d.). https://newtechnetwork.org/

Petrosino, A. J., Lehrer, R., & Schauble, L. (2003). Structuring error and experimental variation as distribution in the fourth grade. *Mathematical Thinking and Learning, 5*(2–3), 131–156.

Schroeder, C. M., Scott, T. P., Tolson, H., Huang, T. Y., & Lee, Y. H. (2007). A meta-analysis of national research: Effects of teaching strategies on student achievement in science in the United States. *Journal of Research in Science Teaching, 44*(10), 1436–1460.

Solomon, G. (2003). Project-based learning: A primer. *Technology and Learning–Dayton, 23*(6), 20-20.

Springer, L., Stanne, M. E., & Donovan, S. S. (1999). Effects of small-group learning on undergraduates in science, mathematics, engineering, and technology: A meta-analysis. *Review of Educational Research, 69*(1), 21–51.

Tyler, R. (1949). *Basic principles of curriculum and instruction*. University of Chicago Press.

Vernon, D. T., & Blake, R. L. (1993). Does problem-based learning work? A meta-analysis of evaluative research. *Academic Medicine, 68*(7), 550–563.

Wright, M. C., Bergom, I., & Bartholomew, T. (2019). Decreased class size, increased active learning? Intended and enacted teaching strategies in smaller classes. *Active Learning in Higher Education, 20*(1), 51–62. https://doi.org/10.1177/1469787417735607

CHAPTER 3

SIX MAJOR ELEMENTS OF PBI

In the first two chapters, we discussed the history of PBI, its theoretical foundations in situated inquiry and communities of practice, how it is differentiated from other instructional approaches, and how it is related to critical content and process standards for K–12 STEM learning. We also discussed why PBI is an effective approach to help students meet these standards and gain an integrated understanding of STEM principles. In this chapter, we discuss the six key elements that make up PBI: (a) a driving question or design challenge, (b) situated or anchored inquiry, (c) collaboration and community, (d) scaffolding and tools, (e) a learner product, and (f) continuous and learning-focused assessment. These six elements are summarized in Figure 3.1 and reflect "Big P" projects as defined below.

ELEMENTS OF "BIG P" PROJECTS FOR PBI

Not every project that is enacted in schools necessarily includes all the characteristics outlined in Figure 3.1. In fact, one of the coauthors (Petrosino) of this book coined the terms "Big P" and "'little p" to denote variability in PBI methods. "Little p" refers to a project that has limited or partial elements of an educational project based on guidelines set out by PBI theorists, such as Brigid Barron and Joseph Krajcik (e.g., Barron et al., 1990; Krajcik et al., 1998). According to Petrosino, "little p" projects lack attributes such as appropriate goals and objectives, necessary scaffolding, and social structures that promote participatory practices amongst communities—they lack elements listed in Figure 3.1.

In one relevant research study (Marshall et al., 2010), preservice teachers' conceptions of PBI were contrasted against conceptions published

Figure 3.1

Six Key Elements of Project-Based Instruction

Driving Question or Design Challenge
- Feasible
- Worthy
- Meaningful
- Generative
- Standards-based
- Ethical & safe
- Integrated

Situated/Anchored Inquiry
- "Real life" situations
- Authentic practice in the discipline
- Grounded in students' experiences
- Draws upon students' funds of knowledge from home and community
- Anchor videos can be created to launch PBI unit

Collaboration and Community
- Involves effective collaboration skills and individual accountability
- Includes argumentation, discussion, mutual respect, and risk-taking
- Group roles can be assigned
- Connections to community sites
- Connections to homes/families
- Connections to STEM practitioners and other community members

Scaffolding and Tools
- 5E Lesson Plans (Engage, Explore, Explain, Elaborate, Evaluate) provide ready-made structure for scaffolding
- Consider support for STEM integration
- "In the moment" scaffolding through identification, projection, coordination
- Gestures as scaffolds
- Technology as a scaffold – environment for exploration, reference material, collaboration, and management

Learner Product
- Often tangible – bridge, catapult, artwork
- Sometimes a plan, design, argument or a presentation
- Not an "ends in and of itself" – focus on concepts the product embodies
- Evaluation of product – teachers, community members, etc.
- Create rubrics for products
- Give opportunities to revise

Assessment
- Formative assessment aimed at continuous feedback, revision, and improvement
- Peer and audience assessment
- Summative assessments (e.g., tests, final product)
- Use of rubrics – make sure students understand, and even give them a role in their design

in educational research. The investigation reported findings that preservice teachers' notions of PBI frequently reflected superficial elements, or what Petrosino has labelled "little p" project aspects. These superficial elements include using unqualified labels or themes for projects without specifying the nature of the inquiry, lacking a proper project implementation plan, and including PBI characteristics in a unit, such as group work and extended time frames, but failing to specify how these aspects could improve the unit. The study found that education publications were more inclined to describe PBI as possessing driving questions, tangible product outcomes, student-driven complex tasks, scaffolding, formative assessment, and cognitive tools which are more in line with "Big P" ideals.

"Big P" projects contain a ***driving question***, one that is tangible, ***situated***, contextualized and meaningful to the students. As students work towards a solution to their driving question, the teacher provides ***scaffolds*** that will help them through this process. Scaffolding is defined in many forms, and includes having students work with technology or using embedded teaching (Barron et al., 1998) techniques to provide students with ideas and hints. In a "Big P" classroom, subject matter content is delivered to students in a "just-in-time" or "as-needed" manner. The theory behind embedded teaching is that information should be provided to students to address a specific problem being faced in hopes of increasing knowledge retention levels. "Big P" projects contain multiple opportunities for formative ***assessment*** (including self-assessment) and revision. Teachers continually check progress throughout the Project life cycle versus proving only summative assessments at the end of a unit. Students would work ***collaboratively*** and communicate with each other and with the community at large. Some scholars (e.g., Barron et al., 1998) suggested having the students present their final ***products*** to peers and a panel of experts on the subject matter, providing students with a sense of agency and social responsibility in their work.

Although many activities in school settings are termed "projects," the six elements in Figure 3.1 truly define PBI (with a "Big P"). Each of these elements is necessary to successfully carry out the complex task of teaching through extended, situated, inquiry-based Projects. If even one of these elements is missing, it can compromise the entire learning sequence for students—indeed, imagine trying to do a challenging project in any professional STEM field without a clear goal in mind, without effective collaboration, or without continuous support and feedback. Students need all of these elements as they pursue STEM Projects at school, too. When planning for a Project-based unit, it is important that educators consider each of these elements carefully and think about how they fit together to form a complete instructional picture.

In this chapter we will discuss each of these elements in turn. However, before moving to the six elements of PBI, we provide a brief introduction to the Engage-Explore-Explain-Elaborate-Evaluate (5-E) lesson plan model. Although the 5-E model is not the only format for PBI lessons, much of the book is presented with this lesson plan format as the context. For this reason, we give a brief background on it before moving forwards.

THE 5-E LESSON MODEL

One lesson plan template that can provide structure for PBI lessons is the 5-E model for instruction (Bybee et al., 2006). In the first phase of a 5-E lesson, the teacher **Engages** students by hooking their attention using a relevant, accessible launch like an anchor video, and interactive story, a puzzling demonstration, a news article or video, and so on. The engagement foreshadows the focus of the day's investigation and serves to get students interested and invested in pursuing the solution to a compelling problem.

In the second phase of a 5-E lesson, students **Explore** a compelling problem, phenomenon, or issue, often in small groups. Students should be given a relatively well-defined task to investigate and provided with tools they may need to approach the problem in different ways. The teacher should provide "just-in-time" support for students' investigations.

In the third phase of a 5-E lesson, students **Explain** what they have concluded from their explorations, often in presentations to the class. The role of the teacher is to facilitate a discussion where these concepts are made explicit and identified for the class using proper, precise mathematical or scientific terminology.

In the fourth phase of a 5-E lesson, students engage in a related activity where they **Elaborate** and deepen their understanding of the STEM principles that are the focus of the lesson. In this phase, students now have a better grasp of the basic ideas of the lesson, and they have been introduced to appropriate terminology to discuss and express those ideas. This phase may be a key opportunity for students to revise their thinking based on the feedback they received and the discussion that ensued during the Explain portion of the lesson.

In the final phase of a 5-E lesson, students and the teacher **Evaluate** the work that has been done by assessing their understanding and their progress towards achieving the lesson's goals. An important point when using this lesson plan format is that although Evaluate is the final phase of the lesson, formative assessment should be happening throughout all five phases of the lesson. For this reason, the examples of 5-E lessons we provide in Chapter 4 include Evaluation sections at the end of each of the 5-Es. These evaluations may be smaller and more informal than the Evaluation that occurs as the fifth "E" in the 5-E lesson, but they are still critical for the teacher to have a clear idea of how students' understanding is progressing and to give timely feedback.

Although the 5-E lesson plan format is a useful way to structure students' Project-based investigations, there are certainly other lesson plan formats that can be used. For example, in elementary mathematics, there is the simpler but somewhat similar "Before/During/After" lesson plan format (Van de Walle et al., 2013). In this lesson plan format, the teacher activates students' prior knowledge and engages students in the Before phase, structures and provides scaffolding for their investigation in the During phase, and facilitates a classroom discussion to formalize concepts and assess student learning in the After phase. In engineering education, lesson plan formats that are design cycles—like the STAR Legacy cycle—are more common (Schwartz et al., 1999).

Developed by researchers at the Vanderbilt-Northwestern-Harvard-MIT Engineering Research Center (VaNTH ERC), the Legacy Cycle (Schwartz et al., 1999) is an inquiry cycle that organizes resources and lessons in projects to motivate and engage learners in investigative activities that model the manner in which researchers approach and solve problems. Sometimes referred to as "challenge-based instruction," the challenge consists of a set of specific goals and products drive learning. Through engaged, group-based activity and achievement of those goals, learners develop knowledge and skills that are real and develop the practices of disciplinary content experts (i.e., cognitive apprenticeship).

Within each challenge of a Legacy Cycle are six stages, or categories of activities, through which a student or a group progress: the Challenge, Generate Ideas, Multiple Perspectives, Research & Revise, Test Your Mettle, and Go Public. The approach is nonlinear; the nature of the "cycle" affords the students opportunities to look forward to see what is next, or loop back to review or revise work based on newly acquired understanding.

Benefits of the Legacy Cycle include affording learners opportunities to understand the nonlinear manner in which complex problems are often approached and ultimately solved. Supporting NGSS Science and Engineering Practices, learning is collaborative in nature and often enhanced by technology. Like many project-based approaches, the Legacy Cycle helps develop college-readiness skills such as note-taking, research, collaboration, as well as oral and written communication. The approach also encourages and supports peer-to-peer mentoring and models the manner in which researcher work on investigative projects. The external scaffold of the Legacy Cycle provides structure to help learners model the problem-solving activity and procedures of disciplinary content experts.

For engineering design challenges, the Project's lessons may follow an overall, macro format for how they fit together. For example, the "Learning by Design" format for Projects (Kolodner et al., 2003) is an important model for how to structure students' inquiry and provide scaffolding in a complete Project-based unit. In this format, students are presented with a design challenge where they plan, test, present, and refine their product, while also engaging in making and investigating different hypotheses. This is similar to the STAR Legacy Cycle (Schwartz et al., 1999) where students are given a design challenge and generate ideas and research the challenge before designing, testing, and presenting their solution. These formats both have key opportunities for scaffolding built in—including opportunities for students to test and revise their design; opportunities for students to discuss, plan, and revise their ideas with others; and opportunities to ensure that students understand the task.

We have two reasons for focusing more on 5-E lessons in this book. First, these lessons are quite prevalent in science education. Although they are less widespread in technology, engineering, or mathematics education, this format is widely applicable across science domains. Second, 5-E lessons are powerful for integrated PBI because they hit all six of our key elements of PBI. The Engage phase connects well to the idea of anchored or situated instruction, as well as providing a hook that promotes participation and understanding at the beginning of a lesson by introducing a driving question. The Explore phase clarifies that teachers should not be directly communicating content—rather, students should be using collaboration and community to learn concepts on their own terms with teacher scaffolding and other cognitive tools. The fact that this part of the format forces teachers to reconsider and move away from traditional teacher-led instruction makes it particularly appropriate for the transformation that implementing PBI involves. Similarly, the Explain phase makes it clear that the students, and not the teacher, should be in charge of developing and explaining conceptual ideas—although again, scaffolding is paramount. The Elaborate phase often gives student groups an important opportunity to apply concepts they just learned to the specifics of a learner product they are working on for their Project, making it ideal for PBI environments. Finally, all PBI lessons need summative assessment in addition to continuous formative assessment—thus the importance of the Evaluate phase.

When determining what lesson plan format to use, teachers should consider the fitness of inquiry in their content area (science, technology, engineering, or mathematics) and consider how the degree of complexity of the lesson format relates to their grade level and their level of expertise. They should also consider the degree to which the lesson plan format highlights and forwards the six key elements of PBI (see Figure 3.1). A key consideration is the degree to which students have agency to discover and learn content and are given voice and choice—rather than using Project work as a means to apply teacher-communicated information. As described in the framework and research results presented by Kapur (2016), learning is most effective when it involves *productive struggle*—when students are given the freedom to explore, fail, reason, and revise based on scaffolding—rather than when instruction is delivered through direct instruction or unguided discovery.

It is also important to consider that a project-based unit will be composed of a number of 5-E or other format lessons that are strung together in a meaningful sequence to build student knowledge. Each of the lessons should fit together to illuminate and support key aspects of the students' inquiry at different points during the life of the Project. We make a distinction between two important types of lessons: benchmark lessons and investigation lessons. Investigation lessons allow students to explore a problem or phenomena in a relatively open-ended manner, promoting student agency and decision-making in how the key STEM concepts unfold. These lessons allow students to make progress in meeting the overall Project goal by allowing them to engage in exploration of the Project concepts as they arise while solving problems and completing tasks. For example, in a Project involving designing a sports field for athletes with special needs, an investigation lesson may involve students researching and creating their group's first scale drawing of the field using geometric constructions with minimal guidance or instruction.

In contrast, benchmark lessons (Singer et al., 2000) are facilitated by the teacher and serve as key points during the Project-based unit where students need a formal introduction to STEM concepts in order to be able to continue their work. These lessons may involve substantial teacher scaffolding of student knowledge and even direct instruction from the teacher. For example, in a Project involving building balsa wood bridges that maximize the strength-to-weight ratio, an investigation lesson may have students construct sketches of their bridge designs based on researching different bridge designs used in the world, and a follow-up benchmark lesson may involve students learning how the physical phenomenon of tension and compression will impact the strength of their designs from a teacher-delivered mini-lecture. In this way, the investigation lessons create a "time for telling" (Schwartz & Bransford, 1998) where there is scientific knowledge the students need to continue in their Project, and they are made to recognize the need for learning academic concepts through benchmark lessons.

Now that we have discussed lesson plan structure in general, we move to discussing the six key elements of PBI.

PBI ELEMENT 1: FORMULATING A DRIVING QUESTION OR DESIGN CHALLENGE

Every effective Project is both launched and sustained by an appropriate driving question or design challenge that sets the overarching goals of the activities. While a *driving question* is posed in the form of an inquiry that students are trying to answer (e.g., How can we measure changes in weather patterns in our community?), a *design challenge* is sometimes posed simply as a need from a client (e.g., design a net-zero sustainable "tiny house" that two people could inhabit). An example of a model for instruction that utilizes design challenges is the STAR Legacy Cycle (Schwartz et al., 1999). In this model, students are presented with a design challenge. The students then generate ideas, investigate multiple perspectives, research and revise, and finally "test their mettle" through experimentation before "going public" and presenting their product. Creating an effective driving question or design challenge is one of the most challenging aspects of PBI, and it often involves significant collaboration, discussion, and revision among those involved in the design of the Project-based unit.

The Source of a Driving Question

An important consideration, then, is the *source* of a driving question or design challenge. Depending on the age, developmental readiness, and background of the students, as well as the goals and experiences of the teacher, a driving question or design challenge can be student-formulated, teacher-formulated, or brought forward through an external client or community member. Often, the most effective model is to codevelop driving questions among teachers and students or among teachers, students, and community members. Teachers have the clearest idea about state and national standards their students must meet as well as the challenges and struggles that their particular students will have in meeting those standards and negotiating Project work. Teams of grade-level teachers who teach the same subject or across STEM fields can collaboratively develop driving questions or design challenges that help them to meet their learning goals for students, with each teacher's unique expertise and experience with students contributing to the design of an effective question.

However, students' perspectives on a driving question are critical as well. A driving question that connects to students' interests, experiences, and prior knowledge while also capturing their imagination and curiosity must be developed with input from the students in mind. Indeed, recent research has touted the importance of "personalized learning" where instruction is "tailored to the specific interests of different learners" (U.S. Department of Education, 2010, p. 12). PBI approaches that involve students in the creation of the driving question or design challenge, drawing from their experiences, could be considered a kind of hyperpersonalized approach to instruction where students are able to take significant ownership of their learning and exercise choice and control. Indeed, recent cognitive research has supported the importance of learner control (Linnenbrink-Garcia et al., 2013; Patall, 2013; Potvin & Hasni, 2014).

A final group that may have significant input into driving questions or design challenges are members of the community—including local businesspeople, community leaders, and concerned citizens, including families of students. All of these people bring in expertise about community needs and issues that the students and teachers may not be aware of, along with the various logistical, ethical, and practical constraints that come along with meeting these challenges. Having a driving question or design challenge that is cogenerated by community members can lend a sense of importance and significance to a Project-based unit and allow students to feel connected to and like they are making a difference in their community. For example, Gutstein (2006) discussed mathematics Projects his middle school students engaged in where they investigated the cost of housing, income, and the allocation of jobs in their community.

Characteristics of a Successful Driving Question or Design Challenge

Several important characteristics make for a successful driving question or design challenge for PBI, which we have gleaned from many years of supporting students in carrying out Project-based inquiries. At its heart, developing an effective driving question is a complex balancing act where many considerations which may naturally conflict with each other must simultaneously be brought to bear. These tensions are inherent to PBI, and significant teacher pedagogical expertise is needed to understand how to weigh each of these characteristics and consider how each will impact the learning of students in a particular classroom.

First, driving questions must be *feasible*, meaning that they can be realistically carried out by your group of students, in their school setting, with the financial, material, and intellectual resources that you have access to. For example, a driving question that involves a close-up examination of volcanoes or glaciers might only be feasible in a very small number of communities, whereas a driving question that involves water or air quality may be feasible anywhere in the world. If your community does have unique affordances such as access to a coastline with a unique ecosystem, a museum specializing in geometric art, or a strong partnership with a robotics company or financial firm, then these can be important drivers when considering what Projects make sense for your school.

Another important aspect of feasibility is whether the students have the technical skills or financial resources to carry out the driving question or design challenge. For example, it may be unrealistic to have elementary students build a net-zero house or to redesign their school to be more energy efficient, but design software can simulate these situations without the feasibility constraints involved in construction. That is not to say that there are no benefits to working with tangible materials in physical space—research certainly has suggested such benefits (Evangelou et al., 2010; Glenberg et al., 2007). Yet, these considerations must be carefully balanced with feasibility. A final consideration for feasibility is the amount of instructional time you plan to devote to the Project—some investigations, while exciting to you and your students, may simply take too much time to complete in a meaningful way. Thus, planning for a Project involves a careful consideration of how long addressing the driving questions will take and an elaboration of each subtask students will need to complete along the way.

A second important characteristic of a driving question is whether or not it is *worthy*—whether it is an important use of your students' time, effort, and imagination. Like feasibility, worthiness can vary greatly from context to context, and what might be worthy to one classroom may be trivial to another. For a driving question to be worthy, it must confront an important issue to the students, to the community, or to the world. It may be most worthy if it involves an issue that is unsolved—where students could not simply Google the answer or optimal solution. However, driving questions that connect to key historical inquiries may also be intriguing to students, such as a Project where students explore different historical proofs of the Pythagorean Theorem; decide which are most convincing, understandable, and aesthetically beautiful; and critically examine how the contributions of different cultures are valued in Western mathematics.

Worthy questions also lie at the heart of disciplines like STEM—or even better, at the heart of multiple disciplines. They may reflect enduring challenges or curiosities that people of the current generation face while also breaking down these challenges into small, manageable pieces that can be meaningfully confronted by a group of students of a particular grade level. This represents the important tradeoff between worthiness and feasibility. An example of worthy challenges currently faced by professional engineers in the 21st century is given in the 14 "Engineering Grand Challenges" (see http://www.engineeringchallenges.org/; Ellis, 2008). Worthy tasks may also reflect key principles in STEM disciplines which are central to understanding the "big ideas" that link many individual concepts, standards, and grade levels together—such as proportional reasoning in mathematics or unity and diversity in biology.

A third important characteristic of a driving question is whether it is *meaningful*—whether it is important and understandable to the students who will ultimately be pursuing it. A driving question involving, for example, an investigation of the nitrogen cycle may be both feasible and worthy for high school students studying biology. However, without the question being explicitly posed to capture how management of the nitrogen cycle is critical to their lives and the longevity of their planet, it may be abstract and distant from their current concerns. An important way to promote meaningful questions and challenges is to involve students in the design of PBI units and allow them to have input into the investigations their class will be doing. However, driving questions that are teacher-generated but carefully scaffolded to reveal their relevance to students' lives and experiences can make a topic that might not have initially been popular become meaningful to students, while also expanding students' horizons and allowing them to become involved in important concerns and challenges related to STEM in the community. A meaningful driving question will thus be posed in a way such that it is provocative to students; it will capture their interest and make them want to figure out a way of confronting the challenge or problem.

A fourth important characteristic of a driving question or design challenge is that it must be ***open-ended and generative***. A driving question that has a simple yes/no answer or could be answered in just a few sentences is not a question that will sustain students' authentic inquiry. Likewise, a design challenge that leaves open only one possibility for the final product of the design is not an open-ended challenge. There must be many different approaches and methods student groups can use to confront the driving question or design challenge so that each student can take ownership and come to understand the investigation in his or her own way. A good driving question must also be generative—it must allow students to generate relevant and important subquestions or subinvestigations that will allow them to specialize in one particular aspect of the investigation and gain deep knowledge of particular areas that they can disseminate to other student groups. PBI is most effective when each Project being completed by class members looks different, while still capturing the same overarching grade-level standards and big ideas of the discipline. This way, students can learn from the work others are doing and feel they are making a meaningful and unique contribution. Balancing generativity with feasibility can be challenging—students may not be ready to complete a Project that has a lot of different avenues for exploration, and they may get confused or overwhelmed if a driving question is too open-ended.

A fifth important characteristic of a driving question is its ***connection to grade-level state and national standards***. This is perhaps the most important quality of a good driving question, and it is also the characteristic that is most likely to be in tension with many of the other characteristics we have discussed. When designing or codesigning driving questions or design challenges, teachers must start with the standards in mind—whether their own unique state standards or national standards like the NGSS or CCSS. Every day that students engage in Project activities, their inquiries should be firmly anchored to standards for their grade level that describe the particular mathematical or scientific concepts they are expected to learn. Further, it is important to connect Projects to process standards as well as content standards. For example, the NGSS include eight practices for science and engineering that cut across all grade levels, including "planning and carrying out investigations" and "engaging in argument from evidence." Similarly, the CCSS for Mathematics include eight standards for mathematical practice, such as "model with mathematics" and "use appropriate tools strategically." Such practice or process standards could be seen as a mortar that holds the bricks that are content standards together in a PBI unit.

Matching a driving question appropriately to grade-level standards can be challenging, as will be detailed later on. Staying true to standards means that educators may need to limit the open-endedness and generativity of a driving question in some situations and in other situations, reject driving questions that, despite being worthy and meaningful, do not connect adequately to grade-level standards. Selecting driving questions or design challenges that are situated within grade-level standards also may limit the extent to which students and community members can take a large role in the development of the inquiries of the class—they may wish to pursue topics that are outside of the standards intended to be covered, or that are too advanced or basic. Further, it can become increasingly difficult to find problems meaningful and relevant to adolescent students, as upper level STEM concepts become more abstract and theoretical.

A sixth important characteristic of a driving question or design challenge is that it be both ***ethical and safe*** for students to pursue. For example, in biology, meaningful investigations involving living organisms may have questionable ethical implications when examined closely. In addition, it must be considered whether the investigation might alienate or cause discomfort for particular learners. For example, a popular Project in mathematics classrooms might be to track calories, exercise, and body weight as it changes over time and come up with a health plan based on the results; however, given the widely known issues adolescents have with body image, requiring students to participate in such a Project, especially in a public manner, involves key ethical considerations. Another important dimension of ethics is whether or not your classroom is a safe and appropriate place for students who have different viewpoints and backgrounds to pursue provocative and controversial ideas in STEM. For example, Projects regarding evolution, ethical treatment of animal test subjects, stem cell research, GMOs, or nuclear power might involve emotionally and spiritually charged issues for some students and must be handled with sensitivity. Finally, it is important that carrying out a driving question be safe for all learners— whether it be a consideration of the safety of the necessary chemicals and substances involved, the power tools that would be used, or the physical environment or ecosystem where students would need to travel.

A seventh and final important characteristic of a driving question or design challenge is the ***potential it offers for STEM integration***. Although not every driving question or design challenge needs to involve multiple STEM fields, many of the most worthy, provocative, and meaningful ones will. Just as STEM integration can allow students to better make meaning of STEM knowledge, enhancing conceptual understanding of and interest in STEM (NRC, 2014), many of the most effective driving questions will involve some level of STEM integration. For example, most Projects that involve collecting data on natural phenomena—such as weather, water quality, or change in an organism over time—will necessarily include mathematics concepts related to measurement. Likewise, many design challenges where students must build physical objects to accomplish a goal (such as a catapult to project an object a certain distance) will involve concepts from geometry and algebra to create and evaluate prototypes. As an example at the elementary level, the National-Science-Foundation-funded City Technology website (www.citytechnology.org) gives a variety of integrated STEM projects for kindergarten through Grade 5, including a project about pop-up books that integrates mathematical concepts with science and engineering concepts like force, motion, and simple machines. As the facilitation of integrated STEM Projects involves significant teacher expertise and for a variety of supports to be provided for students, integrating STEM fields may have important tensions with the feasibility of the Project. In addition, when integrating across STEM subjects, the standards that the Project ties to must be considered for each discipline to ensure that students will be learning grade-level-appropriate content.

Examples of Driving Questions and Design Challenges

In this section, we provide examples of both driving questions and design challenges for Project-based STEM, articulating how each may meet or fail to meet our seven key characteristics. However, as all of the characteristics are heavily context dependent, some driving questions that are appropriate and worthwhile in some contexts may be inappropriate in others. We discuss examples in elementary, middle, and high school grade levels.

In an elementary mathematics class, an example of a poor driving question might be "How do architects determine how big rooms should be?" This driving question is vague and is not well situated in the everyday experiences and concerns of younger children. It is also not clear what the immediate value or application of answering the question would be, although such an abstract question may be more suitable for older students. An example of a better driving question for elementary students might be "Why are the hallways and rooms so overcrowded at our school, compared to other nearby schools?" Indeed, Turner and Strawhun (2005) described elementary students engaging in this project, and they discussed how it connected well to students' everyday experiences and struggles at their school. The culminating event of the project was children presenting their findings to school district administrators—thus the Project had important applications for social justice and authentic mathematical application.

In a middle school science class, an example of a poor driving question might be "Why do birds have hollow bones?" This question is extremely narrow and has a relatively closed-ended, known answer. It is not a particularly worthy question due to its restricted nature, and it may not be meaningful to learners not already interested in the biology of birds. A better driving question might be "What biological adaptations allow living things to fly?" This driving question is more generative and taps into humans' natural fascination with flight. It also more explicitly involves key disciplinary ideas in biology like form and function, and it has the potential to integrate biology with the physical sciences.

In a typical high school geometry class, an example of a poor driving question might be "How is geometry used in art?" This question is incredibly broad and may be difficult to tie to appropriate grade-level standards, particularly since the most obvious connections between geometry and art lie at the elementary or middle school level. While the open-ended and generative nature of this question is admirable, depending on the population of learners that are pursuing it, it may leave learners feeling lost as to where to begin the Project and which avenues to investigate. The Project may thus degenerate into students using their time ineffectively. Further, while this question may be meaningful to some students who are especially interested in the technical aspects of art, it is not likely to be provocative and interesting to most or all learners.

A better driving question may be "How are geometric transformations used in the graffiti art we see in our community?" This driving question more squarely focuses students on important grade-level standards relating to geometric principles, and it also narrows down the kinds of art being considered. While this is a compromise in terms of open-endedness and generativity, it allows for a more feasible and standards-based investigation. This question is also automatically more meaningful to students, as it involves their particular community and the sites they see every day. Finally, although neither question involves significant opportunities for STEM integration, the integration of the sciences with the arts is another important opportunity for integration and meaning-making of STEM subjects.

In a high school engineering or physics class, an example of a poor driving question might be "Can we use a catapult to attack soldiers in war?" First, this driving question is framed in a way such that it has a yes/no answer. While it may be meaningful to some students who are particularly interested in combat and warfare, it may alienate others who find these subjects more controversial or distasteful. Further, it may involve safety issues if students will be building models of such catapults, as the driving question explicitly involves the suggestion of violence against humans. The overly provocative nature of this question may distract students from focusing on grade-level standards and key disciplinary ideas (see Walkington, Nathan et al., 2014). Finally, this driving question is somewhat limited in its generativity and open-endedness, due to its simple yes/no framing and specification of both the catapult as the instrument and soldiers as the target.

A better driving question might be "How do different projectile launchers vary in their destructive force and accuracy?" This driving question remains open-ended in that it does not specify a particular type of projectile launcher, while it also focuses students on grade-level standards by giving the two criteria by which launchers will be evaluated—accuracy and force. These criteria involve the integration of mathematics principles with engineering and physical science principles. While this question may be more meaningful to some students than others, it is less likely to alienate some students than the prior driving question and is situated within the accessible and interesting area of launching things with physical motions—something all students have experiences with from playing sports, playing with toys, etc.

Design challenges can also be well designed or poorly conceptualized. Some unique considerations that go into the formulation of design challenges, compared to driving questions, include the importance of considering the client's needs and specifications while also allowing for student generativity. Further, it is important that design challenges offer students opportunities for iteration—to go through several different cycles of design before a final product is reached. Students need to get feedback continuously throughout this process, including from their clients, to ensure they are meeting the expectations that were envisioned.

An example of a poorly formulated design challenge for high school might be "Construct a model bridge that can handle a large load." The goals and criteria for this challenge are vague and, without more detail, students' bridges will not be directly comparable. Students could go in many directions with this challenge. In order for students to think like engineers, they need to be given design challenges that reflect the criteria that engineers must meet with their design work—including efficiency, feasibility, cost effectiveness, aesthetics, safety, etc. In addition, this design challenge may steer students away from considering important scientific ideas in bridge design, like tension and compression, and encourage them to simply build the heaviest and strongest pile of materials they can construct.

A better design challenge might be "Construct a model of a bridge to go over a river in our community that is safe, cost-effective, aesthetically pleasing, and that has a high strength-to-weight ratio." This challenge gives specific criteria that students can use to evaluate and iteratively revise their design, and it allows for more obvious connections to be made to grade-level standards. This challenge also offers more explicit integration of concepts from mathematics (i.e., ratios, costs) and is situated in the meaningful context of creating a bridge that makes sense for their community or town. It is open-ended and generative to the extent that students can choose their materials and design and worthy in that it is a real, important problem of delicate trade-offs that engineers actually face. Table 3.1 summarizes some of the driving questions and design challenges we discussed in this chapter—and describes how they measure up on our seven key elements of a successful driving question.

Table 3.1

Original and Revised Driving Questions/Design Challenges

Initial driving question/ design challenge	Issues with driving question	Revised driving question/ design challenge
How do architects determine how big rooms should be? (elementary school)	Meaningful (not situated in children's experiences), standards-based (mathematical processes unclear)	Why are the hallways and rooms so overcrowded at our school, compared to other nearby schools?
Why do birds have hollow bones? (middle school)	Worthy, generative (too narrow)	What biological adaptations allow living things to fly?
How is geometry used in art? (high school)	Feasible (too broad), standards-based (could go in many directions)	How are geometric transformations used in the graffiti art we see in our community?
Can we use a catapult to attack soldiers in war? (high school)	Ethical/safe (involves violence/attacking)	How do different projectile launchers vary in their destructive force and accuracy?
Construct a model bridge that can handle a large load. (high school)	Meaningful (not situated in community experiences), standards-based (criteria not clear), integrated (math connections unclear)	Construct a model of a bridge to go over a river in our community that is safe, cost-effective, aesthetically-pleasing, and that has a high strength to weight ratio.

Concept Mapping

In the beginning of Project planning when determining a driving questions, teachers should start with the key STEM concepts or ideas they wish to teach. One way that teachers can conceptualize how different lessons of a Project-based unit fit together is by making a concept map of the key STEM ideas students will need to complete the Project. A concept map is a web that shows how different ideas in the lesson are hierarchically and interactively related. An example of a concept map for a geometry PBI unit about designing a skyline for a city is shown in Figure 3.2.

Figure 3.2

Concept Map Illustrating Relationships Between Ideas in a Geometry PBI Unit on Designing a Skyline for a City

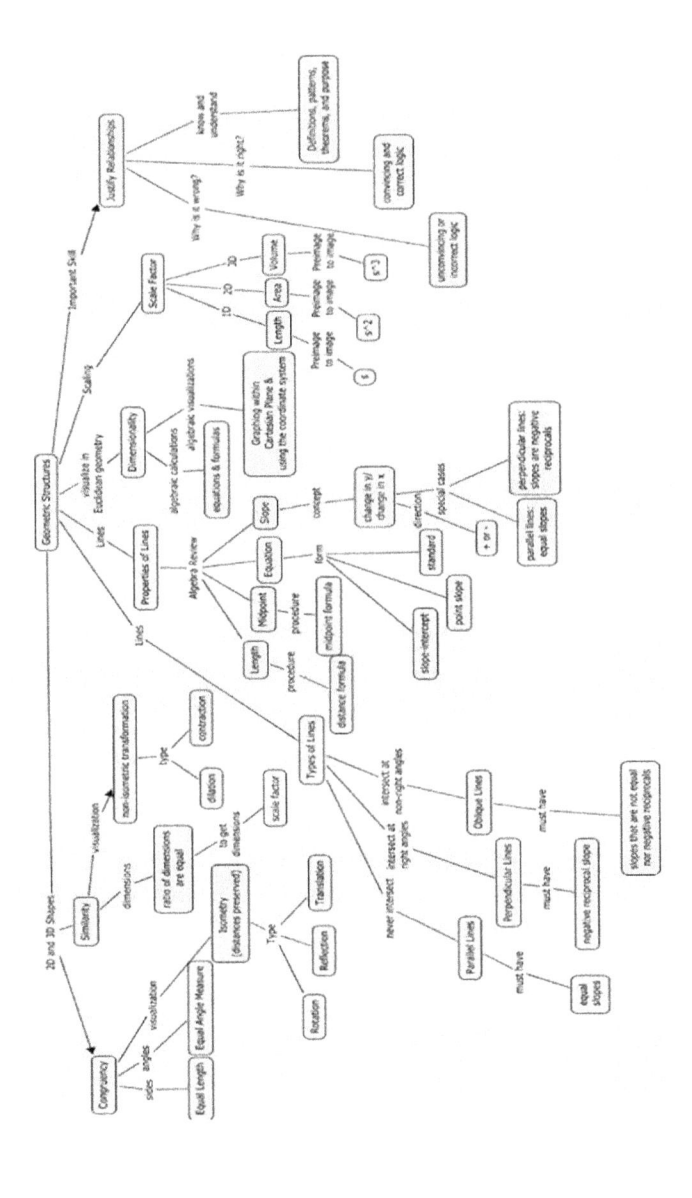

Note. This concept map was taken from UTeach at the University of Texas at Austin and is available online at https://sites.google.com/site/pbiskyline20102/home/concept-map

In this concept map, students are learning about key geometric structures like two and three-dimensional shapes, properties of lines, and scaling, with additional concepts nested within, like similarity and congruency within shapes and midpoint and slope within lines. Mapping out the concepts of a Project-based unit in this matter can help teachers to ensure that there are appropriate benchmark and investigation lessons planned to provide support to students on understanding each key concept. The concept map can help teachers ensure that they are both rigorously covering concepts related to and providing appropriate scaffolding for each part of the Project's goals. The Project-based unit should be designed such that rigor and difficulty build over the sequence of the Project, as does students' expertise using key STEM abstractions, symbols, models, and principles. Concept maps typically have the following properties:

- Help you define what students will need to know and what they will learn during the project
- Describe links between concepts
- Demonstrate a flow or structure
- Show interconnections between all related terms in a web (using verbs)
- Begin to indicate where lessons/investigations might be needed
- Show connections between your primary STEM standards for the time period and your student "deliverables"

PBI ELEMENT 2: SITUATED/ANCHORED INQUIRY

Once a driving question or design challenge has been selected, it is time to present it to students and allow their investigations to get underway. We discussed how driving questions should be meaningful to students, in that they are situated in contexts that they understand, are interested in, and value. This leads to our discussion of the second key element of PBI: situated and/or anchored inquiry. We discuss each of these ideas in turn.

Situated Inquiry

Students' inquiry on a Project is considered "situated" if it occurs in the context of a real-life situation that is problematic or interesting to study. Recall from our previous discussion that situativity theory posits that all learning occurs in the context of students' participation and interactions in social systems like home, school, or their community. In these activity systems, people who participate legitimately in the practices of the system form a *community of practice* that others can join. Hall and Greeno (2008) explained that "concepts and their meanings develop and evolve in settings of practice and are maintained in practices because they are useful in conducting the community's activities" (p. 213). Although school represents its own community of practice with its own norms, standards, and practices, a key goal of PBI is to open students' lives and minds to some of the practices of communities that create new STEM knowledge—namely, those who use STEM to solve real-world problems. This is accomplished by situating students' inquiry within real-world situations where STEM concepts can be meaningfully applied to solve a persistent problem or better understand an important issue. The use of such real-world scenarios that connect to everyday life, home, community, and societal/global communities of practice and/or to the actual professional practices of STEM-focused careers is important for a variety of reasons that are supported by research findings.

Launching a Project that is situated in students' experiences in interacting with the world has the potential to draw upon their *funds of knowledge* (Moll et al., 1992): the understanding students have built through interacting with STEM concepts informally in their home and community lives. Although the versions of these concepts that we encounter and use every day may be substantially different than how the concepts appear in school or academic settings (Lave & Wenger, 1991; Saxe, 1988), thoughtfully designed and carefully discussed connections to funds of knowledge can provide an entry point for students to understand abstract STEM principles (Walkington, 2013; Walkington & Hayata, 2017). For example, students may have significant experience considering mathematical concepts of variation and change as they track their progress in their favorite video game or participate in athletic activities where they keep track of their "stats" as the season progresses (see Walkington, Sherman et al., 2014). Connecting to students' funds of knowledge can allow for STEM ideas to become "grounded" in students' concrete experiences and more strongly connected to prior knowledge, such that they become easier for students to grasp (Goldstone & Son, 2005). Cognitive theory suggests that knowledge that has more connections to other knowledge is more accessible and understandable (Bransford et al., 2000).

Situating Project activities in real-world contexts and concerns also can elicit and maintain students' interest in learning STEM subjects, thus enhancing their motivation for doing STEM. The use of such complex, interesting, and problematic real-world scenarios answers the age-old question for students of "When am I ever going to use this?" Research has shown that students' interest in learning STEM subjects tends to decline over adolescence, particularly (Fredricks & Eccles, 2002; Frenzel et al.,

2010; Speering & Rennie, 1996), as students begin to make the decision that STEM is not for them. However, connections to real-life situations can elicit students' interest (Hidi & Renninger, 2006) in learning STEM concepts, which can become maintained over time. These types of connections can also help students to see the usefulness of learning STEM for their future lives, careers, and goals. Research has shown that when instructional approaches are used that enhance students' conceptions of how useful a subject is, their motivation and academic achievement are improved (Durik & Harackiewicz, 2007; Hulleman et al., 2010; Hulleman & Harackiewicz, 2009).

Clearly, situated inquiry has a variety of benefits for learners, and is often a natural part of PBI. These *learner-centered classrooms* should take into account students' prior knowledge, culture, attitudes, and theories of intelligence (Bransford et al., 2000). However, it is possible to have a Project that is not situated in a real-world context, although these instances will be rare. For example, Projects may involve students exploring the abstract structure of mathematical formalisms and understanding the affordances and limits of different symbolic representational systems. Indeed, the study of abstract mathematical systems can be beautiful and intriguing in its own right, and in advanced mathematics, all knowledge is now necessarily developed with real-world applications in mind.

Anchored Instruction

One specific and widely used method to situate students' inquiry in real-world situations is through anchored instruction. Anchored instruction is a method where a Project is launched by connecting the Project work that will be accomplished to an "anchor," a motivating, complex real-world situation or problem, often presented to students in video format, that will guide and structure students' work on all Project activities. The Cognition and Technology Group at Vanderbilt (1990) described anchored instruction as "environments that permit sustained exploration by students and teachers and enable them to understand the kinds of problems and opportunities that experts in various areas encounter and the knowledge that these experts use as tools" (p. 3). A video-based anchor can be played for students at the beginning of a PBI unit and be utilized to explain the driving question students will be confronting, draw upon their prior knowledge of the subject, and give them useful information and cues about how their investigation will proceed and what data they will use. For example, a Project where students are investigating the physics behind pinball machines might be launched with an anchor video that displays some different pinball machines in action, posing questions about how they work and piquing students' curiosity, while also providing data on the speed and trajectory of the balls in different pinball machines.

Goldman et al. (1994) gave seven key principles for anchored instruction. Anchors communicate information to students using an engaging, narrative format, the story anchors have a generative and open-ended design that allows for student choice, and they include embedded data that can allow students to plan how to approach the problem and make key decisions. Further, the real-world situations described in the anchors are complex, with a multitude of factors that need to be considered, as is the case in real-world problem-solving, and explicit links are provided across different anchored curricula to allow students to make connections. Finally, the use of video allows for information to be given using visual, textual, motion-based, and auditory cues, and multiple anchored episodes are used to facilitate transfer of learned concepts to new situations.

From these principles, we can highlight some of the key characteristics of good versus poor anchor videos. A good anchor video should supply the student with relevant STEM-related information and concepts that can allow them to get started in their Project investigations. The anchor should define an intriguing problem and get students excited about pursuing the Project investigation, while also tapping into their prior knowledge and experience with the topic to allow for multiple points of entry. The anchor video should focus students on the important STEM principles from the start—rather than overaccentuating the "fun" aspects of the Project at the expense of the learning opportunities. Finally, the anchor video should evoke questions rather than give answers; it should neither compromise the generativity of the Project-based task nor "give away" what an optimal solution or product might be.

A well-known example of anchored instruction being used in PBI is the *Adventures of Jasper Woodbury* series. This series embeds complex situations that involve middle grade mathematics concepts into engaging, video-based stories where learners are confronted with problems like rescuing an eagle from a meadow, building a playground and ball field for a vacant lot, or developing a business plan. These videos contain actors depicting different characters in engaging, narrative stories, and they are embedded with the quantitative information students need to solve the problems. Another example of anchored instruction in mathematics is Dan Meyer's 3 act math lessons (http://blog.mrmeyer.com/category/3acts/). These lessons use short video clips to show a mathematical phenomenon or problem (like showing paint being mixed, a canister being filled with water, different arrangements of packaging, or different paths being walked) that gives students an intriguing problem to figure out.

However, anchors do not necessarily need to be in video format. For example, Moses and Cobb (2001) described a Project that algebra students engaged in where they participated in an anchoring event of taking a trip on a subway. They used this event to guide and structure an extended investigation of the number line and positive and negative integers. In the *Engineering Is Elementary Curriculum* (www.eie.org), an elementary school project on designing hand pollinators is launched by an anchoring event of reading a story book *Mariana Becomes a Butterfly*.

PBI ELEMENT 3: COLLABORATION AND COMMUNITY

Collaboration is considered a philosophy of how to relate to others and deal with people in a way that is respectful, involves shared leadership, and leverages the knowledge bases that different collaborators bring to bear (Woolfolk, 2015). Cooperative learning, then, is the act of working with other people to jointly pursue a shared goal or outcome. Note that although "group work" is often synonymous with collaboration or cooperation, simply placing students in groups does not guarantee these behaviors will emerge. Collaboration and cooperation are the hallmarks of most creative workspaces. The skills that relate to collaborating with peers and supervisors are skills that future employers are likely to expect. Cooperative learning is a method of teaching and learning in which students team together to explore a significant question or create a meaningful Project (Smith & MacGregor, 1992).

Establishing an environment that is collaborative can help students meet the English Language Arts Common Core Standards for Listening and Speaking, which detail student-to-student collaboration skills that range from kindergarten to high school. The elementary standards detail how students must engage in conversations where they listen, take turns, stay on-topic, engage in multiple exchanges, ask and answer questions, and express ideas clearly. As students advance to middle school, they should come prepared for discussions, set goals and deadlines, define roles, understand multiple perspectives, delineate arguments and look for appropriate evidence, and use formal English when appropriate. By high school, students should work to justify their views and make new connections based on evidence, actively incorporate group members into discussions, evaluate a speaker's point of view, and honor divergent or creative perspectives. As a teacher, setting up and facilitating an effective collaborative environment can allow students to meet these goals. However, accomplishing this can take quite a bit of work.

Truly collaborative environments in which students feel as if they are part of a productive team will tend to reflect the following:

- Students are actively participating and respect each member of the team and the class.
- All contributions are valued and individuals are not allowed to dominate decision-making or workload.
- Students learn to meet goals as well as deadlines for those goals.
- Students learn to resolve conflicts within their team when they arise.

All of these characteristics of collaborative learning should be discussed, agreed upon and ultimately evaluated using group contacts (see Appendix 3A). As shown in Appendix 3A, it is important for teams to be able to get in touch with each other as needed and to have a clear plan for how they will meet and get Project work done. They should have explicit procedures for meeting the bullets outlined above. Some team conflicts may ultimately not be able to be resolved, and in occasional cases team reorganization may be warranted. Teachers implementing PBI should proactively plan for procedures that would allow a group member to permanently exit a team but still stay meaningfully engaged in the class's activities. An example is given in the "Firing" procedure of the sample group contract.

In order for students to collaborate in a productive manner, certain norms must be put into place to foster true collaboration. These norms include but are not limited to the following:

- Creating respectful, stable and supportive relationships among and between students, teachers, and parents
- Modeling and practicing cooperative learning that then moves into understanding the larger collaborative philosophy
- Opportunities for students to exercise "voice and choice"
- Opportunities for students to take risks learn from mistakes and try again
- All group members are held accountable for the knowledge learned through the Project

These norms set up a working community within the classroom that resembles professional working communities in most STEM fields (Aronson, 2000). The soft skills required for working effectively in these settings can be difficult to measure. It is through collaboration around Projects that those "intangibles" can begin to emerge. Projects give students the opportunity to work in a way that mirrors real-world practices of professionals in the field. Cheng et al. (2008) found that high-quality group processes—including interdependence among group members, individual accountability, equal participation, and effective social communication—were important for students' efficacy during PBI.

An important consideration is how learners should be placed into groups for Project work. Some typical considerations include achievement level in the domain and ensuring that groups are heterogenous in terms of students' prior knowledge level. Groups also might be formulated to bring together students who have different strengths (e.g., artistic, technological, computational, etc.). Alternately, groups might be formulated homogeneously to put students with deeper interest in a subtopic related to the Project together. For example, for a Project on designing accessible sports fields and facilities, all students interested in a particular sport (e.g., basketball) could be grouped together. In addition, social factors should be taken into account; students should be in groups with other students with whom they have no major conflicts and with whom they do not have a history of engaging in extensive off-task behavior. Groups should be heterogeneous with respect to linguistic and cultural background in order to give equal learning opportunities and promote inclusive and respectful attitudes. However, additional supports for collaboration might be needed when language or cultural barriers are particularly high. For example, an LGBT teenager may want group members to address them using a particular pronoun, or a native Spanish-speaking student who has recently immigrated to the United States may want group members to define particular kinds of jargon or popular culture terms. Students should be encouraged to make these desired norms and practices as explicit as possible and create a safe and mutually trusting climate within their group.

In PBI environments, students also may have the opportunity to specialize and work in an area of the Project in which they are particularly interested or knowledgeable. Traditional group roles like leader, material manager, coordinator, etc. may be used; see the group contract in Appendix 3A for examples. Students also may lend different areas of expertise on the Project (e.g., one person leads the computer simulation portions of a Project, while another specializes in physical construction), but cooperation and discussion across students allow for all group members to participate and gain expertise in each area. For example, Penuel et al. (1999) discussed an elementary science project called the Habitats Project, which involved students making physical and virtual models of animal habitats. In the project teams, one student organized research in the library, while another led the web page design and another focused on making HTML tables. Each student was able to take on roles based on what they could authentically contribute to the ongoing activities. In addition, each student in the group "specialized" in one particular animal who lives in the habitats and became a content expert in that animal. This is similar to a "jigsaw" design (Aronson, 2000) where each group member is given a unique piece of the material to learn and becomes the expert on their piece, creating interdependence. In recent jigsaw models, students from each group who are acting as the "expert" in the same topic confer with each other to enhance their understanding and plan ways to teach their group members. The jigsaw design may be especially useful in diverse classrooms that include English language learners, as it creates clear contributions and defined needs for each team member.

Another important aspect of PBI is the role of the local and global communities which inform the project work. Project investigations can be situated within real community sites or concerns—such as investigating the impact of pollution or erosion on community sites, discovering how gerrymandering is used to form political districts in your area, or examining mathematical data about racial profiling of local law enforcement. Before beginning an elementary STEM project on designing a sustainable garden, students might visit community sites like the Farmer's Market; likewise, before beginning a high school project about global warming, students may visit a local science museum. In both cases, the teacher could draw upon experts from these community sites (e.g., the science director of the museum or a botanist at the farmer's market) to enrich students' experiences at the site through their knowledge and perhaps even to continue to support the students throughout their project work. Similarly, via email or teleconferencing software, students can engage with experts from the larger community of STEM practitioners. Some STEM-focused commercial companies encourage outreach and may even allow employees to devote a certain number of work hours per month to STEM outreach. Universities also offer a wealth of expertise students can draw upon—faculty or graduate students can visit school sites and do activities with students, or K–12 students engaged in project work travel to meet with them, perhaps in their labs.

Overall, PBI should take place in *community-centered classrooms* (Bransford et al., 2000). In such classrooms, learning is connected to home practices and students' families, to educational afterschool programs, and to experts from the larger community. Within the classroom community, norms should encourage collaboration, risk-taking, intellectual camaraderie, and argumentation.

PBI ELEMENT 4: SCAFFOLDING AND TOOLS

Once the teacher has made steps to establish a classroom community that is conducive to student–student collaboration, and considered how community-based educational stakeholders can have roles in the Project activities, it is important to consider other ways students can be supported.

The fourth key characteristic of PBI is providing students with important and appropriate scaffolds and tools that they will need to structure their investigation and support their inquiry.

Providing Scaffolds While Planning Project-Based Units

One of the most important ways to provide students with the support they need to be successful in their Project activities is to structure lesson plans to be implemented during the PBI unit. One lesson plan template that provides this structure is the 5-E model for instruction (Bybee et al., 2006), but other lesson plan templates have similar general phases where students are hooked, explore and progressively build knowledge, and then are assessed. In this section, we will talk about the general phases that are typical of many lesson plan formats.

The engagement or hook portion at the beginning of a lesson sequence scaffolds student learning by drawing upon their prior knowledge of the phenomena or problem they will be investigating, providing a meaningful entry point into the activity. For example, during a Project-based unit on the geometry in graffiti art, a teacher might engage students in a lesson on geometric reflections by showing them graffiti images that use reflection in a PowerPoint and asking them what they notice about the designs. Indeed, research has shown that drawing upon students' prior knowledge of STEM principles and prior activity interacting with STEM in their home, community, and world can support future learning (Bransford et al., 2000). In addition, research has suggested that a concreteness-fading approach to instruction is beneficial to student learning, where students begin by tackling concepts in familiar, situated contexts and then gradually transition to working with STEM abstractions(Fyfe et al., 2014).

After the lesson hook, students often have the opportunity to grapple directly with or explore STEM ideas. This often involves discovery learning, and a key distinction when considering discovery learning is the importance of *guided discovery,* where students are provided with scaffolds throughout. Research has suggested that guided discovery is often more effective for learners than unguided discovery without scaffolds (Kapur, 2016). For example, as part of a Project-based unit on circuits, students might be asked to solve a problem involving setting up a voting booth using electric circuits by being given tools like a breadboard kit and circuit simulation software. While the tools themselves provide important structure to the investigation, the teacher should also be ready to scaffold students' exploration through prepared probing questions and by identifying possible student misconceptions and trouble spots that may arise. When issues do arise, the teacher should decide whether to provide scaffolding by providing direct discussion of the issues with students; by encouraging students to talk to their peers, including peers in other groups, to address the problem; or by providing students with additional resources (e.g., an informative site or video, an interactive demonstration, a text, an outside expert) to tackle the problem. In this way, the teacher provides just-in-time support to keep the students from floundering, while not compromising the Project inquiry. For example, the teacher in the circuits lesson may provide students with access to a diagram that shows where pins are located in their integrated circuit for certain issues that arise or may personally look through students' circuit simulation to help them find mistakes in their setup.

Later in a lesson, STEM concepts may begin to be formalized based on student discoveries. Although the students having voice and feeling empowered is critical at this juncture, it is also a key moment for the teacher to provide scaffolding. When students explain their ideas and findings, they may not use canonical STEM vocabulary and concepts in the way they are presented in texts. Indeed, students can often solve STEM problems without actually realizing the science or math they are implicitly doing (Nathan et al., 2017). The teacher also provides such scaffolding by focusing the class's attention on elements of each student's presentation that are particularly unique or critical to understanding these concepts and by comparing and contrasting how different students approached the problem according to meaningful criteria. So, while students provide the "raw material" of an explanation of the relevant STEM principles, it is the teacher who must expertly weave these principles together for the class, building on what students have discovered. For example, in an elementary science lesson where students investigate which factors influence the how a model rocket flies (Lehrer et al., 2001), the teacher may weave into the discussion key terminology like "independent variable" and "dependent variable."

As the lesson sequence progresses, teacher scaffolding might fade. Students should be more empowered to meaningfully investigate and deepen their understanding of the STEM principles through related tasks. For example, in a lesson on biomedical engineering where students investigate the pros and cons of using an insulin pump, during the later phases of the lesson they might explore how the pump would function in specific scenarios where the user is eating different types of meals, engaging in exercise regimens, etc. The teacher's scaffolding would shift to being more detailed and specific as students begin to get into depth about how an insulin pump impacts the systems in the human body.

During the closure of a lesson where student learning is evaluated, the teacher might scaffold students by modelling how they could self-assess and assess the work of peers. The results of the assessments students complete during lesson closure may also be critical to providing scaffolding in future lessons. For example, if the evaluation reveals that many students still hold a key misconception about a scientific principle, providing scaffolding to address that misconception may be a key focus of a future lesson.

A final key consideration when planning how to scaffold learning in a Project-based unit is an explicit consideration of STEM integration. Although the teacher may understand how concepts from science, technology, engineering, and mathematics may all work together to help students complete the Project task, the use of some of these disciplines might be less visible to students. For example, in a Project in science class, students might not recognize the formal mathematics principles they are using to assess their Project (e.g., a strength-to-weight ratio). Similarly, it may be invisible to students when they are acting as engineers when collaborating and planning Project activities and how they are integrating technological principles (like programming and debugging) as they are using software design programs in various ways. It is important that the teacher make moves to explicitly integrate STEM disciplines, making visible to students that they are bringing together ideas from multiple fields. The teacher can do this by planning to use key terms and modelling effective practices from each domain for students and by providing students with resources that allow them to take an integrated perspective.

After Planning—Scaffolding "in the Wild"

Although all of the lesson plan formats discussed here are important tools for planning how learning will be scaffolded during Project-based activities, there is also a tension between too much versus too little planning. Students' activities when engaging in Project-based investigations may organically develop in ways unforeseen by the teacher. Although sometimes it may be the teacher's role to put the students "back on track," in other cases these unexpected turns can be critical opportunities for student learning. Thus, while it is beneficial to plan out significant scaffolding of learning activities for students, teachers should also seek to be flexible and sometimes engage in "discovery teaching" (rather than discovery learning), where they allow the lesson to be partially driven by student needs and voices (Hammer, 1997).

Recent examinations of how STEM teachers provide scaffolding "in the moment" as students are grappling with Project goals have uncovered several important pedagogical moves seen consistently as teachers act (Nathan et al., 2013, 2017; Walkington, Nathan et al., 2014). The use of these pedagogical moves is particularly important when enacting STEM integration, as supporting students in understanding multiple subject areas simultaneously is challenging.

The first pedagogical move for scaffolding STEM lessons is referred to as *identification*. When enacting identification, the teacher gives an explicit canonical name to a key concept or idea that students may be only informally interacting with during their Project. For example, a physics teacher examining students' sketches of ballistic devices they plan to build over the course of a Project-based unit might specifically refer to an angle in the diagram as the "angle of ascent." Later, in a graph that shows the projectile's distance traveled as a function of time, he might use the terminology "rate of change" to describe the line's slope. Identification is important for teachers to remember to enact because often these concepts can remain hidden and implicit to students, although teachers as content experts automatically see how canonical STEM concepts are involved in Project work. This is especially true when STEM integration is being enacted and while multiple content areas are being brought in simultaneously. In this case, it can be a challenge for a teacher to remember and know how to "identify" the key terminology from outside their primary STEM content area. However, this identification allows students to make critical connections between their Project work and the academic STEM field of study. In addition, teachers are not the only ones who can or should use identification—students may spontaneously make connections and identify key concepts or terminology as Project work unfolds, especially if the teacher uses questioning strategies (e.g., What do we call this angle in physics? What do we call the steepness of a line in algebra?) to bring out this knowledge. By supporting students in enacting identification, teachers can ensure that students have ownership of the canonical ideas involved with the Project.

A second pedagogical move that can be used for scaffolding students' Project-based investigations is *coordination*. When students are engaged in PBI, they encounter many different representations of STEM concepts over the life of the Project. For example, in a Project-based unit on bridge building, key concepts related to physical properties of tension and compression are implicit in photos of bridges shown to the class, in design sketches students make using pencil and paper, in free-body diagrams students make showing the different forces, in modeling software that simulates truss design, in large manipulatives the teacher uses to demonstrate how forces affect beams, and finally in the actual wooden bridges the students build. Each of these representations are physically different, and thus can appear dissimilar to learners. Creating a sense of cohesion of the key concepts—here, tension and compression—across all of these disparate forms can be a substantial challenge during PBI. Thus, to enact coordination, the teacher places two of these representations side by side and explicitly links for students how they are related. For example, in a digital electronics unit about designing a voting booth, the teacher coordinated a written truth table with the physical breadboard as he flipped switches on and off while pointing to different entries. Although these two representations of Boolean logic appear to be very dissimilar, by enacting coordination he was able to show students how they were related. In addition, he was able to integrate a mathematical representation with a circuit designed through engineering, enacting STEM integration. Again, however, it is critical that teachers are not the only ones to enact coordination. Teachers can also use questioning and give students tasks that encourage them to make key connections between different representations that occur over the life cycle of the Project. Sometimes, this may involve coordinating representations that occurred at drastically different time points in the Project-based work. This consideration brings us to our final pedagogical move.

The third pedagogical move for scaffolding STEM Projects is *projection*. When a teacher enacts projection, they make a connection backward to an idea or representation that was central during a previous stage of the Project or forward to an idea or representation that students will be building towards over the course of the unit. Research suggests that backward projection can be especially powerful for allowing students to see how the mathematical or scientific formalisms, often introduced as a basis at the beginning of the Project unit, arise in concrete, familiar forms and in designed objects later in the Project as students work to create their product. Often, though, in Project-based units, teachers implement just-in-time learning, where canonical concepts are introduced using benchmark lessons right as students need them to accomplish a step in creating their product. Backward projection can be used to ensure that the central concepts from the STEM fields that are involved in the Project do not become lost and forgotten immediately after the benchmark lesson where they are learned. Forward projection also can be an important tool for letting students know where the Project is going and how each phase of the Project moves them closer to their goal. Nathan et al. (2013) gave an example of a teacher who provided students with an overview of the different representations and concepts their Project-based unit on digital electronics would entail and described how each of the phases of the unit were related using a flow chart organizer. Making these connections can prime learners to better understand how representations and ideas from multiple STEM fields arise and evolve as they work towards designing their final product. Students also can be encouraged to enact projection, particularly backward projection, to generate for themselves how different phases of the Project are linked across time.

Although we have focused mainly on verbal language as a means of providing scaffolding for students during Project-based activities, it is important to note that gestures can serve an important scaffolding purpose. Specifically, when enacting coordination, teachers and learners can use pointing gestures to show how different representations are related.

For example, when coordinating a truth table with a breadboard, pointing to the corresponding parts can allow learners to better understand how the representations are related. Similarly, a teacher could coordinate the different parts of a sketch or a simulation with an actual designed object to show how ideas were transformed during the design process. In addition to pointing gestures, teachers and students use hand or arm gestures that directly model mathematical ideas, such as tilting an arm to show an angle, collapsing the hands to show a bridge collapsing, or tracing geometric shapes in the air to remind students of what they were working on earlier. By invoking or re-invoking STEM ideas through these representational gestures, teachers can give in-the-moment support to students in grasping their meaning through a physical referent. Indeed, a large amount of research has suggested that gestures do help learners to better understand concepts a teacher is trying to communicate (Goldin-Meadow et al., 1999; Valenzeno et al., 2003). In addition, research has suggested that encouraging students to express their ideas through gesture (Cook et al., 2008; Goldin-Meadow, 2005), and using students' gestures as an additional resource to assess their understanding of key STEM concepts, are important pedagogical moves (Williams-Pierce et al., 2017).

Scaffolding for Different Learners

Every teaching context is different, and teachers must understand the kinds of scaffolds that are most appropriate for their students. Scaffolding may differ as a function of grade level—while elementary students may need more cognitive support (in the form of tools, scaffolds, and feedback) to sustain a lengthy and complex Project-based investigation, typically enthusiasm for STEM is higher in the elementary years. Elementary aged students might also need more support in understanding the goals and processes involved in completing a lengthy project, while also keeping track of the "big ideas" in STEM they are trying to learn. By middle school, interest in learning STEM is beginning to decline for many learners (Frenzel et al., 2010; Will, 2017), so students might need motivational support in the form of engaging anchors and hooks; culturally and personally relevant driving questions to answer; and a true sense of ownership, voice, and choice into the Project process. By high school, some students might have deep knowledge of particular STEM areas or be adept at quickly gaining and applying new knowledge through research. These strengths should be leveraged by proactively planning for extensions and additional investigations such students can engage in, while also continuing to provide motivational support for those less interested in STEM.

Students also come to PBI classrooms with language and cultural differences. Scaffolds like visual representations and gestures can be particularly powerful for students who are learning English, as can careful definition and in some cases translation of academic STEM terminology. For both English language learner students and students from diverse cultural backgrounds, a key strategy is also getting to know the student, where they come from, and what their needs are, rather than assuming that they will fit into a particular mold or stereotype. Paying close attention to the simplicity or complexity of the language used in worksheets and other documents that are part of project work can also be important for diverse students, as more complex language can differentially negatively impact these students (Walkington et al., 2018). However, with all of these scaffolds, it is important not to sacrifice the intellectual integrity of the activities for diverse students; they need the same level of challenge and critical thinking as all other students in the classroom. Banks (1994) discussed a framework for multicultural education that outlines various scaffolds that can support diverse students in the classroom—many of which are particularly relevant to PBI. Teachers should integrate different cultures and their cultural knowledge into instruction, examine implicit cultural assumptions of knowledge, and use a variety of pedagogical strategies to reach learners from different backgrounds.

Technology as a Scaffold for PBI

Learning technologies can provide an important scaffold for activities in PBI. Here we discuss three types of technological tools: (a) technology for exploration of STEM concepts, (b) technology for collaboration/Project management, and (c) technology for reference.

One of the most important ways technology can be used as a scaffold during PBI is the use of specialized STEM learning environments where students can engage with and explore key STEM concepts and ideas. One important type is simulation software where students can build virtual prototypes or models and then perform tests on these prototypes or models under different conditions. For example, in engineering, CAD software can simulate the logic of a circuit students plan to build or the forces of tension and compression on a bridge that students are designing. These tools can be invaluable in debugging or revising a planned Project before it is built with materials. In science, students can run simulations of cellular respiration or photosynthesis in which students explore variables that might impact these processes, landing an orbiter on different planets with varying values of gravity (G) or chemical bonding at the atomic level.

In mathematics, students can run simulations of probabilistic events happening repeatedly in software like Tinkerplots, modelling random events in gaming, predator-prey systems, and so on. Software like GeoGebra or Geometer's Sketchpad can allow students to design geometric figures and systems and examine how modifying mathematical aspects of the system—like side lengths and angles—impact the properties of the figures. Other similar software can be used to design two- and three-dimensional objects, floor plans, buildings, etc. Finally, in computer science, software can allow students to explore logic, including loops and if-then statements, as they build and test code in programs like Logo and LEGO Mindstorms. All of these technology tools allow students to test out their ideas in a streamlined, easy-to-use, low-stakes environment and immediately observe a quantifiable result. This gives students significant support in designing a learner product that will best meet the goals of the Project, while also mirroring how the design process often unfolds in real-world contexts.

A second way technology can support PBI is by supporting the collaboration and management of a Project. Video conferencing/calling technology like Google Hangouts can allow students working on Projects to talk to experts who are far away or in the field, getting their input on Project activities. Virtual Project journals, websites, cloud storage, and other organizational and repository tools can provide a place for students to track their progress on the Project in real time, whether or not they are physically at the school. Programs like Google Documents can allow students to collaborate on the planning, designing, and reporting of their Project, with students able to work together on a single document from multiple locations. Teachers can also weigh in, give feedback, and intervene just-in-time by observing the progress students are making using these virtual management tools.

A final way technology can support PBI is through reference material to access STEM content information just-in-time as students need to know something to complete the next phase of their Project. Sites maintained by well-known STEM advocates like the National Aeronautics and Space Administration (NASA), the Smithsonian, Public Broadcasting Station (PBS), Khan Academy, How Stuff Works, WebMD, the Environmental Protection Agency, and the Centers for Disease Control and Prevention have an enormous amount of reference information available on their websites. Apps for phones and tablets are also emerging that have easy-to-access, on-demand reference information for a variety of STEM topics. While much of this reference information is traditionally communicated through text, videos and virtual simulations and demonstrations can help students understand a challenging new concept by using multiple channels, including textual, animated, auditory, and visual information. However, it is important to note that research has demonstrated that students do *not* have particular "learning styles" (Pashler et al., 2008; Rogowsky et al., 2015). While students may express their preference for learning information in an "auditory" and "kinesthetic" manner, research studies have repeatedly shown that honoring these preferences has no effect on learning. However, the important nugget of truth from the learning styles movement is that communicating information in multiple ways is beneficial to *all learners*—regardless of the learning preferences they request.

Scaffolds, through teachers, technology, and other means, are a critical piece of making PBI successful. It is through scaffolding that teachers can facilitate *knowledge-centered classrooms* (Bransford et al., 2000), where the explicit focus is on learning concepts with understanding. This kind of learning supports students in being able to transfer their knowledge to novel problems.

PBI ELEMENT 5: LEARNER PRODUCT

As PBI involves learners investigating driving questions, answering these questions should involve the learner generating a final product that acts as a capstone to their Project activities. The product should reveal to an audience how the learners addressed the driving question, how their investigations drew upon key STEM concepts, and the complex decisions and trade-offs they made as they considered the driving question over time and through different investigations. Learner products are often something tangible that can be built and experienced through the senses—such as constructing a model bridge, a prosthetic limb, or a catapult to fire a ping-pong ball. The importance of aesthetics in such a tangible product can vary—for example, a product of a geometry Project might be a quilt or a piece of MADI (non-representational geometrically abstract) art, whereas an integrated science and engineering Project might involve building an "urban tree" to beautify a downtown area.

In Projects where students are designing a tangible product to solve a real-life problem, the NGSS Standard HSETS1-3, "Evaluate a solution to a complex real-world problem based on prioritized criteria and trade-offs that account for a range of constraints, including cost, safety, reliability, and aesthetics as well as possible social, cultural, and environmental impacts," provides guidance for different ways products can be evaluated. Products can be considered based on their costs—the expense of the material used to build them, as well as the time and human resources involved. In addition, when products are intended for human use, their safety and reliability are of paramount concern. The most efficient solution to a problem may not optimal if it doesn't consider the needs, concerns, and limitations of the humans who will use it. Likewise, students should critically consider how their products would fit into the cultural norms and practices of the society it is designed for, as well as the importance of aesthetics in their final design.

The learner product does not necessarily have to be a physically constructed, tangible object. Sometimes, this may be infeasible financially or logistically, or it may be that spending the classroom time to actually construct the object would not be focused enough on students learning STEM principles to be worth the investment. Thus, learner products can sometimes be plans or designs—such as an elementary school Project where students make a blueprint of a new playground for their neighborhood or a net-zero "tiny house." When students do not actually construct their final product, it is important for the teacher to remind the students of the importance of considering factors like cost and aesthetics and to help the students to predict as much as possible what is realistic and feasible. While these "imagined" products might make more efficient use of limited classroom time, there is an undeniable benefit, as students see their plans realized and construct their product. Much is learned through trial and error in actually constructing a final product, as students discover what is actually feasible and must make difficult trade-offs and decisions that are lost when only a blueprint or plan is made. In addition, constructing an actual object allows that object to be tested—and iteratively revised—which is key to the learning process. Along these same lines, when planning a Project-based unit, it is critical that the teacher takes the time to actually create a sample learner product themselves by doing the Project themselves. When teachers take the time to do this, they learn so many of the nuances and unexpected difficulties that will arise as students work on their product and are in a far better position to anticipate and plan for how to address these issues.

Another type of product that is not tangible is having a Project where students create a model or formulate an argument. For example, a Project in a middle school mathematics classroom might involve students creating a model of how a hotel should determine the price of different rooms. A Project in an elementary school classroom might involve coming up with a standardized process for how crime scene investigators can apply mathematical principles to evidence at a crime scene to help determine the culprit. Creating such a generalized model or process can force students to think beyond the specifics of a particular problem-based scenario and instead consider how STEM principles can be generalized to solve problems with a wide range of parameters. In addition, sometimes the product of a Project might be an argument or a report to an audience. For example, students might engage in a Project where their final product is a presentation to convince an audience about the danger of global warming or about important issues with the placement of liquor stores in their neighborhood

(Tate, 1995), or they uncover and communicate a problem with water quality in their local river and advocate for change. Such Projects can allow students to see how STEM concepts can be a vehicle for social justice and informed citizenship. It can also teach students how to make an argument using evidence and data and how to communicate scientific information to a variety of stakeholders.

When implemented appropriately, the use of a learner product as a culminating task in PBI can help the learner integrate across the different concepts the Project covered, making key connections. The product is the physical instantiation of everything students learned over the course of the Project and critical discussion of and reflection upon the products that various groups present can bring these concepts forward in a personally meaningful manner. Seeing how different groups addressed the same driving question or how different groups addressed their own, related driving questions can allow students to come to a "big picture" understanding of the STEM principles involved. Given the importance of the learner product to the Project cycle, it is critical that these products do not become an end in and of themselves. In particular, especially when there is competition between groups, students can become so focused on their product that they lose track of the STEM principles that are supposed to be the central focus on their activities. For example, in design Projects, students may begin to focus on "building a cool structure" rather than on critically engaging with principles of physics and engineering design. Learner products are most effectively implemented when they are cycles of planning, constructing, testing, reflection, and revising, as well as when learners can compare and discuss their products and get feedback from the teacher, their peers, and knowledgeable others.

An excessive focus on the learner product can also give students a tendency to focus on concrete, salient, and physical forms of STEM principles, while ignoring the abstract, sometimes subtle STEM principles that these products are supposed to embody. For example, Walkington, Nathan, et al. (2014) discussed a STEM classroom where once students started constructing their model bridges during a bridge-building Project, there was little additional discussion of the central science concepts of tension and compression, the learning of which was the purpose of the Project. The bridges the students were building and testing certainly incorporated these concepts, but they were subtle and possibly even invisible to novices in the bridge design. It is important for the teacher to use coordination and projection to remind students of the abstract STEM principles and how they arise in learner products. It is also important that the teacher balances how much they use the product as a motivating force of the Project. If the teacher heavily accentuates that students need to sit through the "boring" theory in order to get to the "fun" part of the Project where they get to build something, it should not be surprising when students have a tendency to leave the theory behind at later stages in the Project. Indeed, as discussed previously, the STEM principles that the Project incorporates should be interwoven in a "just in time" manner, where students realize that they need to understand a new STEM idea in order to make progress in constructing their product. This allows the product to act as a motivating force behind the Project while also keeping the STEM learning goals at the forefront.

An important part of thinking through the product you want students to design as part of your Project-based unit is how that product will ultimately be evaluated and by whom. A common practice is to have students present their products to the class, but teachers can also bring in other staff members and students from the school as well as outside community members and stakeholders with expertise in and commitment to the area the Project covers. Local universities, nonprofits, community advocacy groups, and staff from informal STEM learning sites can all be sources from which to find an external audience to evaluate and give feedback on learner products. All evaluators of learner products should have a clear idea of what the criteria and constraints were for the design of the product and how the teacher communicated that the product would be evaluated. Creating rubrics for learner products, as detailed in the next section, is an important way to organize Project activities from the beginning of the Project cycle and make sure that all learners clearly understand the expectations. Having audience members, including students, come up with critical questions to ask during the product presentations in advance can allow for a richer discussion, particularly if the presence of outside stakeholders may be intimidating to students. Finally, the teachers themselves should carefully consider what questions they wish to ask the groups presenting their products in order to ensure that the underlying STEM principles are being brought to the forefront even at this final stage of the Project cycle.

The presentation of the learner product, however, does not always have to signify the end. Project activities can involve "mini presentations" or even "practice presentations" where students get feedback in order to test and revise their ideas. Ongoing, linked Project-based units can be created where students choose a product they previously created and revise it to meet new criteria or design goals. In addition, in Projects where stakeholders in the audience choose a best design or most optimal solution, this decision can launch a new Project-based unit where the class focuses on the next stage in the development and implementation of their product.

To conclude, perhaps the most challenging aspect of the learner product in PBI is the time commitment involved. Having students spend time building, testing, revising, and presenting their products is far less time efficient than simply having students create a plan that incorporates the

STEM principles and move on. However, the experience of creating and revising a learner product is truly at the heart of PBI, as it is at the heart of the work that real scientists, engineers, and applied mathematicians do as they solve real-world problems. Because it is so time consuming, it is ever important that the teacher takes advantage of every opportunity to focus students on the STEM learning goals and to make explicit the broader STEM-type behaviors (e.g., collaboration, communication, cycles of feedback and revision, community involvement, social justice) that they are embodying as they work towards their goal.

PBI ELEMENT 6: ASSESSMENT

Assessment is ubiquitous and not unique to the classroom setting. PBI is a dynamic process of investigation and collaboration using the same processes and technologies that real scientists, applied mathematicians, and engineers use. With this in mind, it also must be acknowledged that these same professionals are constantly self-assessing their work and having their work evaluated by others. These professionals are held accountable for the quality of their products, protocols, algorithms, or testing results and analysis. STEM professionals evaluate throughout a Project, not just at the end. This type of ongoing assessment allows these same professionals to revise and redesign products or experiments for higher quality outcomes. Assessment and evaluation are part of contributing to the STEM profession. Dynamics of assessment in PBI typically include self-assessment, peer assessment, and teacher or expert assessment. Learning is continuously assessed and lesson structures change in the moment based on student understanding. Both formative assessments aimed at continuous improvement (Black & Wiliam, 2009) and well-structured summative assessments that measure student learning (Harlen, 2005) are important.

Anecdotally, it has been observed that there are those who believe that students will not do well on "THE TEST" if they spend too much time on Projects. In a large study conducted in Detroit Public Schools, Geier et al. (2008) found this to not necessarily be the case. This study illustrated that assessment, usually meaning summative tests, and PBI are not mutually exclusive. Additional recent studies ranging from elementary school to high school have found gains on standardized tests and other student knowledge assessments for students engaged in PBI in STEM (Bicer et al., 2015; Han et al., 2016; Harris et al., 2015; Yoon et al., 2014).

In PBI classrooms, there must be multiple opportunities not only for formative self-assessment but also for revision of projects. We have multiple assessments because we want to check student progress throughout the unit instead of at the end when time has run out and teachers no longer have the opportunity to go back and clear up some of the misconceptions. It is not only important for students to go through the motions of doing the project, but we also want to give them the opportunity to go back and revise. If we skip this very important step in the development of a project, we might leave some misconceptions untouched, and the students will leave the room with those misconceptions. In the real world, many times we find ourselves working in groups, be it a church committee or a board of executives. It is important for students to develop social skills at a young age, including being able to effectively communicate with each other and with the community. This is why students are required to present their final projects both to their peers and, many times, to a panel of experts. This gives them a sense of agency, meaning they take responsibility and pride in their work and therefore try to make it the best they can to impress their audience. Doing these types of projects not only leaves an impression with the student, but also helps them develop an understanding of what they are doing and for what reason.

In well-designed PBI, ongoing assessment is vital and offers the opportunity for students to redesign, revise, and improve just as it does with STEM professionals. This includes formative (immediate), interim, and summative forms of assessment. Without ongoing assessment, the entire process no longer becomes relevant, and a product/Project simply becomes another form of summative assessment and not the learning mechanism. This is not to say that summative assessment should not be included. In fact, it is just the opposite. Summative assessment should be a part of PBI for two basic reasons: It allows for individual accountability even though Projects are collaborative efforts, and it provides for teacher accountability, which is typically a requirement. All assessment needs to be aligned with the learning performances set out by the teacher at the beginning of the Project. We argue that more authentic summative assessments utilize information directly gleaned from student presentations or final products as part of the summative assessment.

Rubrics are useful and utilized to gage quality of performance criteria as well as to set expectations for high-quality work (Bargainnier, 2003). The key to effective use of rubrics in PBI is the creation of all rubrics in the early part of Project development. This allows the instructor to design the Project around the learning goals reflected in the rubrics and to consider how the final product and the assessment go together to demonstrate student learning. Students should be allowed to become familiar with or at least aware of all forms of assessment and utilize them during the Project as a form of self-assessment, peer assessment, and then ultimately used by an expert for the final assessment. Students can have a role in determining how they should be summatively assessed by helping to create and design Project rubrics. The expert who engages in the summative assessment when the time comes is typically the teacher, but it can also include professionals from the community evaluating student products.

Two important aspects to successful assessment in PBI are to decide what needs to be assessed and how each objective will be assessed. A recommendation for achieving this, as stated earlier, is to plan the assessment as the Project is formulated with learning objectives clearly in mind and to create a variety of assessments. Consider using multiple rubrics, quizzes, class discussions (both small groups and whole class), presentations, and written mini-reports. Sources for ideas of varied assessment can be found in Angelo and Cross's (1993) comprehensive handbook *Classroom Assessment Techniques* and Doran et al.'s (1998) *Science Educator's Guide to Assessment*. Angelo and Cross utilized Fink's Taxonomy of Significant Learning, which introduced a taxonomy of significant learning that integrates cognitive and affective areas and adds a metacognitive component. The six types of significant learning are integrated but not hierarchical and may be used selectively depending on the learning outcome desired. They specific areas are (a) Foundational Knowledge: understanding and remembering information and ideas; (b) Application: skills, critical thinking, creative thinking, practical thinking, and managing projects; (c) Integration: connecting information, ideas, perspectives, people, or realms of life; (d) Human Dimension: learning about oneself and others; (e) Caring: developing new feelings, interests, and values; and (f) Learning How to Learn: becoming a better student, inquiring about a subject, becoming a self-directed learner. Doran et al.'s work shows teachers how to give students regular and accurate feedback, reinforce productive learning habits, and help students reflect on their own learning during hands on activities and other skills tasks. For rubric development, see Buck Institute for Education *Project Based Learning Handbook* (Markham, 2003) and Rubi Star rubric design software (http://rubistar.4teachers.org).

Students can also assess each other's performance on the Project, particularly during the final stage of Project works where student groups present. Palinscar and Herrenkohl (2002) described a distribution of peer audience roles for an inquiry science investigation where audience members were given different roles to take. Some audience members were responsible for thinking about the relationship between theory and predictions in the presentations, while others focused on the clarity of the findings, and still others focused on the relationship between theory, predictions, and findings. However, this is not the only approach that can be used to engage in peer evaluation. An example of a peer evaluation form for a Bioethics Project is given in Appendix 3B.

A final issue to address is the role of PBI in a classroom's year-long cycle of content instruction and assessment. In Chapter 1, we initially made the distinction between "projects" (little p) and "Projects" (Big P), with more explanation provided in this chapter. Using a Project as a way for students to apply what they have already learned, and as a creative summative assessment of their learning in a unit, is a perfectly acceptable and useful assessment strategy. However, it is not the kind of "Big P" PBI we are talking about in this book. The PBI we discuss has students actually learn novel concepts *through* and *during* their Project work. The Project is not the assessment—it is the method of teaching. Students are assessed continuously throughout the Project work via formative assessment, and the summative assessment is often their final product or presentation.

Overall, PBI classrooms should be *assessment-centered* (Bransford et al., 2000) in that there is a continuous focus on formative assessment and visible progress monitoring by both teachers and students themselves. In assessment-centered environments, use formative assessment to identify students' preconceptions and misconceptions, assess where students are in the "developmental corridor," and modify their instruction accordingly and provide feedback.

SUMMARY

In this chapter we discussed the six key elements of PBI. PBI should be instigated by a driving question or design challenge that meets criteria like feasibility, worthiness, and generative; it should be situated and anchored in students' experiences in the world, including the world outside of school; it should involve collaboration, cooperation, and connections to community contexts; it should involve significant scaffolding and tools to support complex Project work; it should culminate in a learner product that is authentic and meaningful; and it should involve continuous assessment, including formative assessment, summative assessment, and self-assessment. These six elements are at the core of what differentiates "doing projects" (i.e., "little p") from implementing Project-based instruction (i.e., "Big P"). It is PBI with a "Big P" that is most powerful in transforming students' understanding, perspectives, and learning experiences, as it involves these six important and synergistic instructional practices.

REFERENCES

Angelo, T. A., & Cross, K. P. (1993). *Classroom assessment techniques: A handbook for faculty* (2nd ed.). Jossey-Bass.

Aronson, E. (2000). *Nobody left to hate: Teaching compassion after Columbine*. Macmillan.

Banks, J. A. (1994). *An introduction to multicultural education*. Allyn and Bacon.

Bargainnier, S. (2003). Fundamentals of rubrics. In D. Apple (Ed.), *Faculty guidebook* (pp. 75–78). Pacific Crest.

Barron, B. J., Schwartz, D. L., Vye, N. J., Moore, A., Petrosino, A., Zech, L., & Bransford, J. D. (1998). Doing with understanding: Lessons from research on problem- and project-based learning. *Journal of the Learning Sciences, 7*(3–4), 271–311.

Bicer, A., Navruz, B., Capraro, R. M., Capraro, M. M., Oner, T. A., & Boedeker, P. (2015). STEM schools vs. non-STEM schools: Comparing students' mathematics growth rate on high-stakes test performance. *International Journal of New Trends in Education and Their Implications, 6*(1), 138–150.

Black, P., & Wiliam, D. (2009). Developing the theory of formative assessment. *Educational Assessment, Evaluation and Accountability, 21*(1), 5–31.

Bransford, J. D., Brown, A. L., & Cocking, R. R. (2000). *How people learn: Brain, mind, experience, and school*. National Academies Press.

Brown, J. S., Collins, A., & Duguid, P. (1989). Situated cognition and the culture of learning. *Educational Researcher, 18*(1), 32–42.

Bybee, R. W., Taylor, J. A., Gardner, A., Van Scotter, P., Powell, J. C., Westbrook, A., & Landes, N. (2006). *The BSCS 5E instructional model: Origins, effectiveness, and applications*. Biological Sciences Curriculum Study.

Cheng, W. Y., Lam, S. F., & Chan, C. Y. (2008). When high achievers and low achievers work in the same group: The roles of group heterogeneity and processes in project-based learning. *British Journal of Educational Psychology, 78*(2), 205–221.

Cook, S. W., Mitchell, Z., & Goldin-Meadow, S. (2008). Gesturing makes learning last. *Cognition, 106*(2), 1047–1058.

Cognition and Technology Group at Vanderbilt. (1990). Anchored instruction and its relationship to situated cognition. *Educational Researcher, 19*(6), 2–10.

Doran, R., Chan, F., & Tamir, P. (1998). *Science educator's guide to assessment*. National Science Teachers Association.

Durik, A. M., & Harackiewicz, J. M. (2007). Different strokes for different folks: How individual interest moderates the effects of situational factors on task interest. *Journal of Educational Psychology, 99*(3), 597–610.

Ellis, G. (2008). Grand challenges for engineering. *IEEE Engineering Management Review, 37*(1), 3-3. http://www.engineeringchallenges.org/challenges/16091.aspx

Evangelou, D., Dobbs-Oates, J., Bagiati, A., Liang, S., & Choi, J. Y. (2010). Talking about artifacts: Preschool children's explorations with sketches, stories, and tangible objects. *Early Childhood Research & Practice, 12*(2), 1–16.

Fredricks, J. A., & Eccles, J. S. (2002). Children's competence and value beliefs from childhood through adolescence: Growth trajectories in two male-sex-typed domains. *Developmental Psychology, 38*(4), 519–533.

Frenzel, A. C., Goetz, T., Pekrun, R., & Watt, H. M. (2010). Development of mathematics interest in adolescence: Influences of gender, family, and school context. *Journal of Research on Adolescence, 20*(2), 507–537.

Fyfe, E. R., McNeil, N. M., Son, J. Y., & Goldstone, R. L. (2014). Concreteness fading in mathematics and science instruction: A systematic review. *Educational Psychology Review, 26*(1), 9–25.

Geier, R., Blumenfeld, P. C., Marx, R. W., Krajcik, J. S., Fishman, B., Soloway, E., & Clay-Chambers, J. (2008). Standardized test outcomes for students engaged in inquiry-based science curricula in the context of urban reform. *Journal of Research in Science Teaching*, *45*(8), 922–939.

Glenberg, A. M., Brown, M., & Levin, J. R. (2007). Enhancing comprehension in small reading groups using a manipulation strategy. *Contemporary Educational Psychology*, *32*(3), 389–399.

Goldin-Meadow, S. (2005). *Hearing gesture: How our hands help us Think*. Harvard University Press.

Goldin-Meadow, S., Kim, S., & Singer, M. (1999). What the teacher's hands tell the student's mind about math. *Journal of Educational Psychology*, *91*(4), 720–730.

Goldman, S. R., Petrosino, A., Sherwood, R. D., Garrison, S., Hickey, D. T., Bransford, J. D., & Pellegrino, J. W. (1994). Multimedia environments for enhancing science instruction. In S. Vosniadou, E. De Corte, & H. Mandl (Eds.), *Technology-based learning environments* (pp. 89–96). Springer.

Goldstone, R. L., & Son, J. Y. (2005). The transfer of scientific principles using concrete and idealized simulations. *The Journal of the Learning Sciences*, *14*(1), 69–110.

Gutstein, E. (2006). *Reading and writing the world with mathematics: Toward a pedagogy for social justice*. Taylor & Francis.

Hall, R., & Greeno, J. G. (2008). Conceptual learning. In T. Good (Ed.), *21st century education: A reference handbook* (pp. 212–221). SAGE.

Hammer, D. (1997). Discovery learning and discovery teaching. *Cognition and Instruction*, *15*(4), 485–529.

Han, S., Capraro, R., & Capraro, M. M. (2015). How science, technology, engineering, and mathematics (STEM) project-based learning (PBL) affects high, middle, and low achievers differently: The impact of student factors on achievement. *International Journal of Science and Mathematics Education*, *13*(5), 1089–1113.

Harlen, W. (2005). Teachers' summative practices and assessment for learning–tensions and synergies. *Curriculum Journal*, *16*(2), 207–223.

Harris, C. J., Penuel, W. R., D'Angelo, C. M., DeBarger, A. H., Gallagher, L. P., Kennedy, C. A., Cheng, B. H., & Krajcik, J. S. (2015). Impact of project-based curriculum materials on student learning in science: Results of a randomized controlled trial. *Journal of Research in Science Teaching*, *52*(10), 1362–1385.

Hidi, S., & Renninger, K. A. (2006). The four-phase model of interest development. *Educational Psychologist*, *41*(2), 111–127.

Hulleman, C. S., Godes, O., Hendricks, B. L., & Harackiewicz, J. M. (2010). Enhancing interest and performance with a utility value intervention. *Journal of Educational Psychology*, *102*(4), 880–895.

Hulleman, C. S., & Harackiewicz, J. M. (2009). Promoting interest and performance in high school science classes. *Science*, *326*(5958), 1410–1412.

Kapur, M. (2016). Examining productive failure, productive success, unproductive failure, and unproductive success in learning. *Educational Psychologist*, *51*(2), 289–299.

Kolodner, J. L., Camp, P. J., Crismond, D., Fasse, B., Gray, J., Holbrook, J., & Ryan, M. (2003). Problem-based learning meets case-based reasoning in the middle-school science classroom: Putting learning by design into practice. *The Journal of the Learning Sciences, 12*(4), 495–547.

Krajcik, J., Blumenfeld, P. C., Marx, R. W., Bass, K. M., Fredricks, J., & Soloway, E. (1998). Inquiry in project-based science classrooms: Initial attempts by middle school students. *Journal of the Learning Sciences, 7*(3–4), 313–350.

Lave, J., & Wenger, E. (1991). *Situated learning: Legitimate peripheral participation*. Cambridge University Press.

Lehrer, R., Schauble, L., & Petrosino, A. J. (2001). Reconsidering the role of experiment in science education. In K. Crowley, C. D. Schunn, & T. Okada (Eds.), *Designing for science: Implications from everyday, classroom, and professional settings* (pp. 251–278). Erlbaum.

Linnenbrink-Garcia, L., Patall, E., & Messersmith, E. (2013), Antecedents and consequences of situational interest. *British Journal of Educational Psychology, 83*, 591–614.

Markham, T. (2003). *Project based learning handbook: A guide to standards-focused project based learning for middle and high school teachers*. Buck Institute for Education.

Marshall, J. A., Petrosino, A. J., & Martin, T. (2010). Preservice teachers' conceptions and enactments of project-based instruction. *Journal of Science Education and Technology, 19*(4), 370–386.

Moll, L. C., Amanti, C., Neff, D., & Gonzalez, N. (1992). Funds of knowledge for teaching: Using a qualitative approach to connect homes and classrooms. *Theory into Practice, 31*(2), 132–141.

Moses, R. P., & Cobb, C. E. (2001). *Radical equations: Math literacy and civil rights*. Beacon Press.

Nathan, M., Srisurchan, R., Walkington, C., Wolfgram, M., Williams, C., & Alibali, M. (2013). Cohesion as a mechanism of STEM integration. *Journal of Engineering Education, 102*(1), 77–116.

Nathan, M. J., Wolfgram, M., Srisurichan, R., Walkington, C., & Alibali, M. (2017). Threading mathematics through symbols, sketches, software, silicon and wood: Integrated STEM instruction to produce and maintain cohesion. *The Journal of Educational Research, 110*(3), 272–293. https://doi.org/10.1080/00220671.2017.1287046

National Research Council. (2014). *STEM integration in K–12 education: Status, prospects, and an agenda for research*. National Academies Press. https://doi.org/10.17226/18612

Palincsar, A. S., & Herrenkohl, L. R. (2002). Designing collaborative learning contexts. *Theory Into Practice, 41*(1), 26–32.

Pashler, H., McDaniel, M., Rohrer, D., & Bjork, R. (2008). Learning styles concepts and evidence. *Psychological Science in the Public Interest, 9*(3), 105–119.

Patall, E. A. (2013). Constructing motivation through choice, interest, and interestingness. *Journal of Educational Psychology, 105*(2), 522–534.

Penuel, W. R., Korbak, C., Cole, K. A., & Jump, O. (1999). Imagination, production, and collaboration in project-based learning using multimedia. In C. M. Hoadley & J. Roschelle (Eds.), *Proceedings of the Computer Support for Collaborative Learning (CSCL) 1999 Conference*. International Society of the Learning Sciences.

Potvin, P., & Hasni, A. (2014). Interest, motivation and attitude towards science and technology at K–12 levels: A systematic review of 12 years of educational research. *Studies in Science Education*, *50*(1), 85–129.

Rogowsky, B. A., Calhoun, B. M., & Tallal, P. (2015). Matching learning style to instructional method: Effects on comprehension. *Journal of Educational Psychology*, *107*(1), 64–78.

Saxe, G. (1988). Candy selling and math learning. *Educational Researcher*, *17*(6), 14–21.

Schwartz, D. L., & Bransford, J. D. (1998). A time for telling. *Cognition and Instruction*, *16*(4), 475–523.

Schwartz, D., Lin, X., Brophy, S., & Bransford, J. (1999). Toward the development of flexibly adaptive instructional designs. In C. Reigeluth (Ed.), *Instructional design theories and models* (3rd ed., pp. 183–213). Erlbaum.

Singer, J., Marx, R. W., Krajcik, J., & Clay Chambers, J. (2000). Constructing extended inquiry projects: Curriculum materials for science education reform. *Educational Psychologist*, *35*(3), 165–178. https://doi.org/10.1207/S15326985EP3503_3

Smith, B. L., & MacGregor, J. T. (1992). What is collaborative learning? In A. S. Goodsell, M. R. Maher & V. Tinto (Eds.), *Collaborative learning: A sourcebook for higher education*, (pp. 10–29). National Center on Postsecondary Teaching.

Speering, W., & Rennie, L. (1996). Students' perceptions about science: The impact of transition from primary to secondary school. *Research in Science Education*, *26*(3), 283–298.

Tate, W. F. (1995). Returning to the root: A culturally relevant approach to mathematics pedagogy. *Theory Into Practice*, *34*(3), 166–173.

Turner, E. E., & Strawhun, B. T. F. (2005). "With math, it's like you have more defense": Students investigate overcrowding at their school. In E. Gutstein & B. Peterson (Eds.), *Rethinking mathematics: Teaching social justice by the numbers* (pp. 81–87). Rethinking Schools.

U.S. Department of Education. (2010). *Transforming American education: Learning powered by technology*. http://www.ed.gov/sites/default/files/netp2010.pdf

Valenzeno, L., Alibali, M. W., & Klatzky, R. (2003). Teachers' gestures facilitate students' learning: A lesson in symmetry. *Contemporary Educational Psychology*, *28*(2), 187–204.

Van De Walle, J. A., Karp, K. S., & Bay-Williams, J. M. (2013). *Elementary and middle school mathematics: Teaching developmentally* (8th ed.). Allyn & Bacon.

Walkington, C. (2013). Using learning technologies to personalize instruction to student interests: The impact of relevant contexts on performance and learning outcomes. *Journal of Educational Psychology*, *105*(4), 932–945.

Walkington, C., Clinton, V., & Shivraj, P. (2018). How readability factors are differentially associated with performance for students of different backgrounds when solving math word problems. *American Educational Research Journal, 55*(2), 362–414. https://doi.org/10.3102/0002831217737028

Walkington, C., & Hayata, C. (2017). Designing learning personalized to students' interests: Balancing rich experiences with mathematical goals. *ZDM Mathematics Education, 49*(4), 519–530. https://doi.org/10.1007/s11858-017-0842-z

Walkington, C., Nathan, M., Wolfgram, M., Alibali, M., & Srisurichan, R. (2014). Bridges and barriers to constructing conceptual cohesion across modalities and temporalities: Challenges of STEM integration in the precollege engineering classroom. In S. Purzer, J. Strobel, & M. Cardella (Eds.) *Engineering in pre-college settings: Research into practice* (pp. 183–210). Purdue University Press.

Walkington, C., Sherman, M., & Howell, E. (2014). Personalized learning in algebra. *Mathematics Teacher, 108*(4), 272–279.

Will, M. (2017, June 8). Most students are not naturally interested in STEM, teacher say. *Education Week.* http://blogs.edweek.org/teachers/teaching_now/2017/06/how_can_teachers_get_students_interested_in_science_and_math.html

Williams-Pierce, C. C., Pier, E., Walkington, C., Clinton, V., Boncoddo, R., Nathan, M., & Alibali, M. (2017). What we say and how we do: Action, gesture, and language in proving. *Journal for Research in Mathematics Education, 48*(3), 248–260.

Woolfolk, A. (2015). *Educational psychology* (13th ed.). Pearson Education Inc.

Yoon, S. Y., Dyehouse, M., Lucietto, A. M., Diefes-Dux, H. A., & Capobianco, B. M. (2014). The effects of integrated science, technology, and engineering education on elementary students' knowledge and identity development. *School Science and Mathematics, 114*(8), 380–391.

APPENDIX 3A:

Sample Group Contract for Collaboration

Group Name:	Period:
Name of Project:	

Section 1: Contact Information and Planned Meeting Time(s)

As a group, we agree to keep in contact with each other on this Project.

Name	Phone	Email

Decide within your group on a day and time that you could meet outside of class on a regular basis (typically once a week) to work on your PBI Final Project.

Day:_____ Time:_____ Location:_____

Section 2: Our Roadmap for Sharing Responsibility Within Our Group

- What are our group goals?
- How will we work together and delegate tasks appropriately?
- How will we hold each other accountable?
- How will we make sure that everyone in the group is learning the knowledge and skills from the group participants?
- How will we monitor our progress?
- How will we overcome setbacks?
- How will we celebrate our successes?

Section 3: Firing Procedure

Should a group member repeatedly choose not to uphold this contract, we will follow this procedure in order to fire him or her from our group. Firing a member may result in you taking on their work. The extent to which you accrue extra work will be determined after Step IV below. Your grade is determined by your work and participation towards the Project, but not the quality of the Project as a whole.

1. They will receive one verbal warning.
2. They will receive two warnings that will be both verbal and written (e-mail). The emails will be sent to the teacher as well as the group member.
3. After the second warning, the group will have a conference with the instructors discussing the problem and how it can be resolved.
4. Upon the next violation of the contract, the group will seek instructor approval to fire their group member. If the instructor approves, the group member is fired.

Group members who are fired may NOT take any work with them from their group. They will start over from the beginning with the Project. They may be hired by another group if all group members in the new group give consent.

Section 4: Agreement

We have read this group contract and agree to uphold the standards that we have set for ourselves. We will monitor not only our own behavior but also that of our group members. We understand that it is our responsibility to enforce this contract.

Signed:

Section 5: Addendum (Group Roles)

Group Leader: _____

This person will be responsible for organizing group communications to include: proposing solutions and new directions for creative expression, communicating group questions, concerns, and progress to the teacher, and for communicating teacher comments and instructions to the team.

What strategies will the group leader use to fulfill the responsibilities above?

Materials Manager: _____

This person will take responsibility for keeping up with all group work materials, storing it such that said materials are accessible to all group materials are accessible to any/all group members, and for note-taking during all group meetings. The person will create a plan for completion and setting deadlines for the group to follow and ensure that all materials are submitted in the proper format.

What strategies will the materials manager use to fulfill the responsibilities above?

Coordinator: _____

This person will take responsibility for clearly defining the relationship between ideas and facts of research utilized in Project, offering new ideas and avenues of research, maintaining teamwork and cooperation through enforcing group contract, and monitoring group mood and atmosphere whenever a problem arises or group energy lags.

What strategies will the coordinator use to fulfill the responsibilities above?

APPENDIX 3B

Bioethics "Legacy Challenge" Peer Review

The rubric below outlines the criteria for the Legacy Challenge presentation presented in the "Go Public" step. Use the rubric to evaluate the presentation of the group you are reviewing. Once you have completed the chart, answer the questions at the bottom. You should look over the chart and the questions before reviewing the presentation.

Presentation Criteria	Description	Points Possible	Points Awarded	Suggestions for Revision
Length	Presentation length should be between 5 and 10 minutes.	10 points		
Quality of Visuals	This category includes the appropriateness of the font size, color, and graphics. Could you see all aspects of the presentation clearly?	30 points		
Ideas Clearly Communicated	Did you understand the points that the presenters were making? Were their ideas well organized and articulated?	30 points		
Level of Support for Ideas	Was their argument convincing? Was their opinion well supported? Was there support for each idea presented?	30 points		
	TOTAL POINTS	100		

Peer Review Questions: *Remember your responses should be detailed enough to help the group make useful revisions.*

1. Did this group convince you of their position on Dr. Barton's proposal?
2. If so, which point of their argument did you find the most persuasive? If not, what did you disagree with and why were you not convinced?

3. Was each point in the argument supported by evidence? If not, which point/s did you think was/were not well supported?
4. Did you think that the presenters had a deep understanding of the ideas they were presenting? Were they confident and well informed? Explain your answer.
5. Were the PowerPoint slides well done? Were the font, color, and graphics appropriate? What did you like the best? What did you not like?
6. Was the presentation interesting? Did it hold your attention? If not, what suggestions can you give?

CHAPTER 4

PUTTING YOUR PROJECT TOGETHER

In Chapter 3, we discussed the six key elements of PBI and some of the research and theory that these elements are built on. In this chapter, we focus on practices for actual implementation of Projects in STEM classrooms. We return to the key elements, but in a way that aims towards the practicality of putting a Project-based unit together. We describe seven steps in the process of planning a Project-based unit:

1. Determining your project time frame
2. Starting with the end in mind
3. Considering students' prior knowledge
4. Forming your driving question
5. Designing a Project anchor/launch and planning for student engagement
6. Creating benchmark and investigation lesson plans
7. Planning formative and summative assessment during the Project

STEP 1: DETERMINING YOUR PROJECT TIME FRAME

A common question concerning PBI is "How long should I make the unit?" In some ways this question often reminds us of when a student asks how many pages they should write for a research paper. A common response is usually something like "long enough to answer your research question"—this often provokes a frustrated look from the students who are seeking a clear and concise answer, such as "15 pages double-spaced APA format." However, after we give the answer. "Long enough to answer your research question," we should help unpack what this means and clarify the components we hope are covered as they begin their research paper. In a similar fashion, we believe a PBI unit can be anywhere from about 2 weeks to a semester or even longer, provided the Project covers our six major elements from Chapter 3. In general, we have found it challenging to implement our sense of a "Big P" project in less than 2 weeks (or roughly eight class meetings of approximately 50 minutes). Why might this be?

A Project has a driving question or problem that serves to organize and drive activities, which amounts to a meaningful project and a culminating product or multiple representations as a series of artifacts (Krajcik & Czerniak, 2014). A Project also has a consequential task that meaningfully addresses the driving question (Brown & Campione, 1994). To specify this point, we must take a close look at four of our key elements that facilitate the use of PBI in K–12 classrooms:

1. A driving question that is anchored in a real-world problem and ideally integrates multiple content areas
2. Opportunities for students to make active and situated investigations that enable them to learn concepts, apply information, and represent their knowledge in a variety of ways
3. Collaboration among students, teachers, and others in the community so that knowledge can be shared and distributed between the members of the learning community
4. The use of cognitive tools in learning environments that support students in the representation of their ideas: cognitive tools such as computer-based laboratories, hypermedia, graphing applications, and telecommunications (Blumenfeld et al., 1991).

As can be seen from the elements above, at its core, PBI emphasizes learning activities that are long-term, interdisciplinary, and student-centered. Unlike traditional, teacher-led classroom activities, students often must organize their own work and manage their own time in a Project-based class. PBI differs from traditional inquiry by its emphasis on students' collaborative or individual artifact construction to represent what is being learned. It is important to realize, however, that as students become more familiar and accustomed to Project-based classrooms, their comfortableness with the components of PBI become more streamlined. Less time is spent on the various components of PBI and more time is spent on the investigative activities of the Project itself. In general, while it is true that Projects take time, it is arguably time well spent. A Project is not meant to "cover" a long list of standards but rather to teach selected important standards in greater depth. We have found that a Project often covers more standards than originally intended since there is an organic nature to a Project.

When implemented well, PBI gives students the opportunity to explore problems and challenges that have real-world applications, thus increasing the possibility of long-term retention of skills and concepts. However, we also need to create and maintain the space and time for these student interactions to occur and be nurtured. Being too much of a "task manager" can have unintentional negative consequences for the type of environment we seek with PBI. It is important to manage it well, so time is used efficiently, but it is also important to give the Project space to develop and be nurtured. A Project is more than a series of successive class lessons. Therefore, it often requires a shift by the teacher in terms of thinking about the tension between effectiveness and efficiency. Yet, not all Projects need to take months to complete. Perhaps most importantly, a teacher does not need to use PBI all the time; one or two Projects a year is much better than none at all.

Some teachers are concerned that planning a project takes too much time. PBI does require significant advance preparation, but planning Projects gets easier with practice. You can also save planning time by collaborating with other teachers, sharing Projects, adapting Projects from other sources, and running the same Project again in later years. In essence, a shift to PBI represents a shift in focus from

> the discrete to the complex, from the predictive to the relational, and from the linear and determinant to the self-generating and indeterminant. Empiricism and rationalism are giving way to a post-modern reappraisal of how we think and how we develop and create knowledge. Project based instruction transforms curriculum from its deep roots in predictable, Tyler inspired modernism to a post-modern paradigm that requires new and different ways of thinking and will not be an easy transition. In societies characterized by advanced technology and complex social dynamics which did not exist at the time modernity was emerging, a post-modernism approach to pedagogy and curriculum planning will result in new ways of thinking and different perspectives indicative of a world that is changing before our eyes. (Stuever, 2009, p. 89)

STEP 2: STARTING WITH THE END IN MIND

We have had significant success in working with both pre- and in-service teachers, whom we will call project designers, utilizing a variation on reverse design or reverse engineering (Wiggins & McTighe, 1998). Instructors and classroom instructional designers often approach a project design in a linear, forward manner, meaning they consider how to teach the content, develop assessments around activities, and then attempt to draw connections to the learning goals of the project or of the course. We embrace the backward design approach where instructors first consider the learning goals of the project, of course. These learning goals then include the learning goals instructors want their students to have learned when the project is concluded. As the learning goals are established, the next stage considers issues of assessment. The backward design framework helps the instructors consider these overarching goals and how students' knowledge acquisition and skill development will be evaluated before consideration is given to how to teach the content. Thus, backward design is a much more intentional approach to course design than traditional methods of project design.

We believe it is important to initially think about the end in mind in order to have a clear understanding of what is to be accomplished instructionally during the project. This means to have a sense of where you are going in order to better understand where you are and the steps needed to take to get where you are going. Recall our discussion about the Legacy Cycle, which acts as an external scaffold to help in this process for instructional designers and students alike. One must be careful however that having the end in mind should not stifle productive instructional detours that may occur during a project or be mistaken that any deviation from the end goals is unproductive instructionally. We encourage Project designers to consider what final product or activity could students produce or complete that would adequately answer the driving question. In addition, we ask them to try and complete that activity or produce that product themselves at least partially. We find that this exercise helps to structure the Project, particularly helping to identify where benchmark and investigation lessons, sometimes referred to as "workshops," will be most needed to produce a just-in-time learning experience. Finally, we have found that if designers go through multiple iterations with peer feedback, with peers often referred to as "critical friends," the final products are ultimately stronger and more refined Projects.

Thinking about what students might "do" as a culminating deliverable for a project is often one of the more difficult steps in project planning. We often brainstorm with designers about different options that come to mind when thinking about their driving question. We also encourage them to do the same with their students. It is powerful for students to determine for themselves the most effective way to answer the driving question. One of the activities that we engage in is "What would a professional do?" We ask the designers to think about the professional that would be engaged in answering a question similar to theirs. What would that professional need to do, create, or communicate with to address the question at hand? Examples of final deliverables might include one or more of the following:

- A research paper or poster
- A formal proposal
- A scaled model
- A proposed design
- A persuasive letter to an official entity
- A stakeholders meeting
- A computer model or simulation
- A debate
- A public service announcement
- An informational pamphlet

For example, in learning about solubility and dissolution, students explored a nearby cavern, collected data, made observations and then prepared a data-driven argument as part of a stakeholders meeting for the county. The final product included a research paper presenting and explaining the student findings, as well as a presentation designed to persuade a county agency how best to utilize the newfound resource in the form of a cavern. Each type of final deliverable requires designers to decide upon criteria and an evaluative rubric to guide their students. This resembles the process of evaluating RFPs (request for proposals) in many STEM fields as well as government and industry.

At each stage of the project design process, we have designers share ideas and critique each other's work in order to revise and refine their designs. These sessions of collaboration where peers are referred to as "critical friends" are important not only for the designers but, as mentioned earlier, it can be a useful tool for students as they progress through the Project themselves.

Some key questions for teachers to ask themselves when planning each day of their Project-based unit are these:

1. What do I want the students to know or be able to do? (Standards, "students will be able to…")
2. How will the students show me they know or can do these things? (artifact/activity/rubrics)
3. How can I help the students get them to where I want them to be? (lessons, investigating, data collection)

Answering these questions for different portions of the Project activities can result in a Project sketch that outlines the students' trajectory of activities. However, simply using this framework for approaching a multiple-day Project sketch does not ensure that teachers who are planning will fully understand the purpose and cognitive effort required to develop their lesson at the start. The initial Project sketch is a storyboard that needs to be thoroughly developed. Falling into the trap of using the sketch as a document that is sequentially filled out should be avoided.

Although the teacher does significant advance planning of a PBI unit, it is important to remember that students can be responsible for the creation of both the driving question and the activities used to address the driving questions, as well as the nature of the artifacts they create as their learner product. Additionally, teachers or curriculum developers can create questions and activities. Regardless of who generates it, the driving question cannot be so constrained that outcomes are predetermined, leaving students with little opportunity to develop their own approaches to investigating and answering the initial question.

Student freedom to generate artifacts is critical, because it is through this process of generation that students construct their own knowledge. Because artifacts are concrete and explicit (e.g., a model, report, consequential task, videotape, or film), they can be shared and critiqued. This allows others to provide feedback, makes the activity authentic, and permits learners to reflect on and extend their knowledge and revise their artifacts. The artifacts are a concrete representation of the learning goals of the Project; they demonstrate the knowledge the student has accumulated over the course of the Project.

Projects are decidedly different from conventional activities that are designed to help students learn information in the absence of a driving question. Such conventional activities might relate to each other and help students learn curricular content but, without the presence of a driving question, they do not hold the same promise that learning will occur as do activities orchestrated in the service of an important intellectual purpose (Sizer, 1984). Supporters of PBI claim that as students investigate and seek resolutions to problems, they acquire an understanding of key principles and concepts (Blumenfeld et al., 1991). PBI also places students in realistic, contextualized problem-solving environments (Cognition and Technology Group at Vanderbilt, 1992). These kinds of practices allow for learning goals that emphasize deep, conceptual understanding of STEM principles.

STEP 3: CONSIDERING STUDENTS' PRIOR KNOWLEDGE

Since the late 1990s, STEM educators have acknowledged the importance of using formative assessments and diagnostic tools to improve student learning and teacher pedagogy. Important research-based publications, such as the NRC's *How People Learn: Brain, Mind, Experience, and School* (Bransford et al., 2000), increased instructors' understanding of the importance in identifying the prior understandings that students bring to the science classroom and using these preconceptions as springboards for learning.

It is now accepted and documented that students come to class with a wide range of preexisting knowledge, attitudes, and beliefs that impact how they attune, make sense of, and organize information. How students integrate and process new information impacts how they may remember, categorize, use, and create new knowledge. We know that new knowledge and skill is related to preexisting knowledge and skill. Therefore, understanding what students know or can do about a particular problem, concept, or idea can assist us in developing instructional activities that build off the strengths of students and may possibly help in addressing weaknesses in their full understanding or explanation of phenomena.

We call the activity that assesses prior knowledge and skill *formative assessment*, which was discussed as the sixth key element of PBI in Chapter 3. Formative assessment—or assessment for learning—has been touted by research as the single most effective strategy for advancing learning for all students. And while it is true that formative assessment has been incorporated by an increasing number of instructors into their classroom practices, many of these same teachers are discovering that the process is more complex than simply administering a question probe or checking in with students to see if they understand what is taking place in their Project. Teachers are finding that to use assessment results to further learning, strategies must be carefully linked to specific learning goals. As Jim Minstrell (1992) said, teachers see the importance of asking students two critical questions: What do you know, and how do you know that? Getting answers to these questions are especially important in assessing conceptual learning (as opposed to assessing skill mastery) in STEM learning. It is also essential when planning a Project-based unit to understand what knowledge your students already have and where they need to go.

One attribute of formative assessment is that we quickly see there is often a range of potential responses from students and that these responses can help inform the instructor about next steps. Are the formative assessment results uniform? Do responses fall into a few different categories? For example, if most of the students in class have more naïve or weak understanding of a concept that is critical to a deep understanding of the field, we may decide to cover it in a specific lesson, provide some supplementary instruction, or offer outside resources for the students to utilize. Conversely, if most students show proficiency and understanding in a skill or concept you were planning to cover, you may decide to either not spend as much time on the concept, skip it all together, or delve for a deeper understanding. Another attribute of formative assessment is that if individual students lack some of the prerequisite knowledge and skills needed for a course, they could be informed or required to take some prerequisite coursework, or at least be told of the need to develop proficiency in areas on their own if they are to do well in the course. All of these considerations should feed into the planning of a Project-based unit.

There are several different methods to assess preexisting knowledge via formative assessment. Some are direct measures such as traditional tests, concept maps, portfolios, debates, etc., and others are more indirect such as reflections, self-reports, inventory of prior courses and experiences, and so on. Below are some methods that instructors involved with UTeach at The University of Texas at Austin and elsewhere have employed.

Concept inventories are multiple-choice or short-answer tests that target fundamental concepts within a domain. These tests are designed to uncover systematic misconceptions. For instance, the Force Concept Inventory (Hestenes & Wells, 1992) is a test designed for students who have received some formal instruction on physics and is meant to assess conceptual understanding rather than quantitative skills.

Self-assessment probes are indirect methods of assessment that ask students to reflect and comment on their level of knowledge and skill across a range of items. These items can include knowledge and skills that are prerequisites for the course, as well as items that will be addressed in the course.

Concept-map activities (Novak & Cañas, 2006) can reveal the underlying structure or organization of students' knowledge of a concept or group of concepts. These are very helpful when the kinds of causal theories and relations among ideas are critical to students' understanding of course materials. According to Krajcik and Czerniak (2014), based on the work of Joseph Novak, concept maps

> provide visual external representations of the relationships among concepts and can be used as tools to empower learners by making them aware of their own thinking.... Using concept maps before a project starts to elicit students' initial understandings, providing a baseline. During a project, students can use concept maps to track the concepts they are learning and to integrate them with prior understandings.... By comparing earlier versions of their concept maps with later versions, students see how their conceptual understandings are developing. Additionally, students can compare their concept maps with those of other students in order to see the connections formed ... sparking new connections for themselves. Concept maps developed at the end of a project help students tie together all the concepts explored and serve as a form of assessment. (p. 292)

STEP 4: PUTTING YOUR DRIVING QUESTION TOGETHER

Once the goals for student learning have been established and you have a clear picture of students' prior knowledge, it is time to determine your driving question. To this end, we have found several successful suggestions over the years. One must begin with a study of the curriculum standards and student outcomes to be addressed during the time frame for the proposed PBI unit. Next, we have found it beneficial to write down a number of driving questions that might address the content, student essential skills, and knowledge that are significant AND address these curriculum standards. Following this activity, we then have our designers list multiple student investigations that might serve to address these driving questions, as well as the content and curricular standards. At this point, Project-based designers, together with their team, can best determine which investigations are feasible for the students. Once these steps have been accomplished, we must now consider how to contextualize the Project by starting with a well-constructed problem-based scenario that will introduce the driving question and provide basic skills and knowledge that set students up for success with the more open-ended Project-based unit that follows (Barron et al., 1998).

At this point, we have worked on developing a series of design questions that have proven to be beneficial in order to evaluate the quality of the driving question and its relationship to the lessons planned. Specifically, designers of the Project-based unit should be able to have a handle on what STEM content the students will learn. They should know which STEM content standards will be met during the Project. Designers should have an idea through existing literature on cognitive development in the content areas as to whether or not the students can generate their own subquestions.

As the Project develops, designers need to have a sense of what feasible investigations students will do during the Project. Some of these investigations should be initially designed, but we have also found that other investigations become apparent only after the unit is actually implemented or has gone through multiple iterations. Designers of these units need to be aware of two related questions: How is the driving question anchored in the real world, and, closely related to that, how can the driving question be made meaningful for students? Again, it is important to emphasize that these questions have both a scaffolding nature as well as a reflective and iterative nature. Scaffolding with these questions will help the novice Project-based designer tie the driving question to the rest of the Project. Our initial attempt to answer these questions are often close approximations that can only be refined after the driving questions has been implemented into a Project. Questions can then be refined once the designer reflects on realized or missed opportunities and any unanticipated student generated questions as well as the critical importance of iteration.

Ultimately the true test of the driving question for a successful Project is whether or not the driving question can sustain student engagement as well as significant development over time (Krajcik et al., 1999). Chapter 3 provides significant guidance on what characteristics a good driving question has and how driving questions can be generated for STEM areas.

STEP 5: DESIGNING A PROJECT ANCHOR/LAUNCH AND PLANNING FOR ENGAGEMENT

Anchor Videos

One of the ways to support open-ended Projects is to provide help for students and teachers to continually reflect on how and why their current activities are relevant to the overall goals or the "big picture" of the project. One of the primary strategies we have used to scaffold children's efforts with the sometimes challenging, open-ended nature of Projects has been to begin with a video or anchor that sets up the problem or driving question and then leads the students into the Project.

The launch video provides a big picture without the complexity often associated with open-ended projects. Our version of a launch video is similar to problem-based learning (see Cognition and Technology Group at Vanderbilt, 1992; Williams, 1992) and involves the use of authentic but sometimes simulated problems that students and teachers can explore collaboratively. The influence of these launch videos originates with the Learning Technology Center and the Jasper Woodbury and Scientists in Action Problem Solving Series as an example of problem-based learning environments (Center for Technology Transfer & Commercialization, n.d.). Each of these problem-based series consists of multiple video-based or animated anchor stories. The stories follow a narrative structure with one exception: They do not end with a conclusion but rather with a challenge for the students who are watching. All the information needed to meet the challenge is included in the story as well as some information that is not necessarily related to solving the problem. In contrast, PBI experiences are typically centered in everyday settings with tangible outcomes. For instance, we treat actively monitoring a river as Project-based, whereas working with a simulated, river emergency in a video is problem-based. Additional examples include constructing a playhouse for a community center as opposed to designing in a simulated context or actively planning and carrying out a fun fair at school versus planning for an imaginary fair.

Frameworks for Integrated Project-Based Instruction in STEM Disciplines   95

As students design their launch video, we try to establish a set of five design principles that leverage previous work on anchored videos (Petrosino & Koehler, 2007). First, we want to be sure to emphasize a driving question that would support generativity. We want to see the video support generativity by being generative in design. That is, it led the viewer to think about problems and subproblems that are in the launch video and the problems students will be solving have more than one right answer. Second, the launch video employs embedded data in order to generate problem-solving goals, find relevant information, and engage in reasoned decision-making. A third design principle is that the launch video supports problem complexity and scaffolding or guidance. A good launch video presents problems that are complex and require multiple steps to solve. The launch video should be helpful in guiding the students through a complex project. A good launch video must include engaging and relevant video content to keep the attention of the intended students as well as provide an interesting narrative or storyline for an age appropriate audience. Finally, a good launch video must be technically good. The sound quality, visual quality, and text as well as narration must all be readable and understandable.

Student Engagement in PBI

We are often asked about how to motivate students to learn in PBI. Motivating students to learn is one of the primary concerns of the preservice teachers we prepare as well as many of the more experienced teachers we work with in the field. In general, we have found in our decades of work that student motivation has never been a major concern when enacting well-designed Project-based units. We attribute this conclusion to a few factors including: a motivating driving question; a complex problem rich enough to support sustained inquiry over time; opportunities to collaborate with fellow students as well as experts in the field; instructional scaffolds that help support student learning; and the opportunity to be assessed using traditional assessments as well as some novel assessments such as presentations, debates, challenges, and the creation of learning artifacts.

However, we do not intend to trivialize the issue. We understand this is a real concern and that there is a great desire for "guarantees" on how to keep students engaged and motivated during the multiple days, weeks, and sometimes months that a Project may encompass. To that end, we offer some practical advice. Not every student will be fully engaged during every moment of a long-term project. We would argue this is probably a good thing as the students would become exhausted! Rather, we look for sustained engagement over time often enhanced by students pursuing their own questions or investigation. We design our units with the idea of scaffolding inquiry but with a goal of helping students develop, investigate, and pursue their own questions. We also place value on the idea of distributed expertise—essentially, that as the unit is initially developed, each member of the group is critical and important to the knowledge needed to solve the complex problem.

An early account of the work one of the authors and his colleagues conducted in the area of motivation in PBI involving STEM took place at Vanderbilt University and is reported in Barron et al. (1995). In this work, late middle school students were involved in a complex project that required revision, mathematics, graphical representations, and lasted over a month in class. This demanding learning environment led to students working with enthusiasm. Working toward doing or hands-on instruction does not need to reduce student motivation. For instance, students completed multiple rounds of projects where they solved a number of video-based anchors. One of these included a project known as The Big Splash, where students created a business plan for a school carnival.

Student interest and energy continued undeterred throughout the entire time period. To gain a better understanding of student motivation using Projects, a group of the students was interviewed the following fall. The interviews were conducted by people whom the students would not associate with the research group. Interviewers asked the students to think about the previous school year when they were fifth graders and to describe things that made them feel proud and creative (two attributes associated with positive motivation). Interviewers also asked students to name things from the previous school year that they would like to do again. Across the three questions, more than 50% of the students spontaneously mentioned the projects (known as "Jasper," which in their minds included the projects that followed Jasper) as a learning experience that was very special to them in the previous grade. When these students were asked directly about "Jasper" later in the interview, nearly all said that it was a very important experience for them.

Some of the more interesting work in the area of student achievement and motivation using PBI was conducted by our colleague Phyllis Blumenfeld and her colleagues at the University of Michigan. In addition to showing learning gains on curriculum-based pre- and posttests, Blumenfeld also examined student performance on Michigan's state standardized examination, the Michigan Educational Assessment Program. The findings show that students in the Detroit public schools who used at least one designed PBI performed substantially better on the required state science test than a matched group of students who did not use the Project-based materials (Geier et al., 2008). Perhaps even more encouragingly, students who used more than one of the specially designed Project-based units performed significantly better on the state examinations than students who used only one unit. Yet, content knowledge was not the only area of gains for these Detroit public school children. Blumenfeld et al. (2005) showed that students' attitudes in science remained positive. This is a very important finding since the literature reports that students' attitudes toward science typically decrease during the middle school years (Yager & Penick, 1986).

In short, keep students engaged in challenging and complex questions of their own design, allow for a wide variety of assessments and opportunities to be an important part of the collaborative process, and provide proper scaffolds for successful involvement with the complexity of PBI. Student motivation is an important precursor to learning, and therefore, is an important component in any successful PBI classroom. Studies have shown that the more students are engaged in the classroom, the better they will succeed. Several decades of research have shown that students' engagement predicts their learning, grades, achievement, retention, and graduation (NRC, 2004).

A considerable body of research and theory show the positive relationship between student motivation and cognitive engagement (Blumenfeld et al., 1991). One component of PBL that increases motivation is immersing students in real-world situations and real-world problems (Graesser et al., 2002). Unlike traditional instruction which tend to set up problems to be solved in a singular way, PBL allows for flexible thinking and solutions. This engages students in a story which is more memorable than other forms of narrative, especially for students that can be easily distracted. Stories allow students to build inferences and develop higher order and creative thinking (Graesser et al., 2002).

Our experience and those of our colleagues has shown that student motivation and engagement will be enhanced and disruptions to student learning will be at a minimum when students are actively engaged in complex problems and problems in which the context and/or design is somewhat determined by student input and contextualized (Bernacki & Walkington, 2018; Hickey et al., 2001).

Example of Project Launch

We next provide an example of how the Project anchor/launch and a focus on student engagement can come to fruition in the design of the launch of a Project-based unit. We use the Mission to Mars PBI materials, which were developed to be an extended Project-based unit for middle school STEM classrooms.

Description of Mars Video Dilemma. The Mission to Mars dilemma is a 7.23-minute video that prompts the students to generate some of the many problems that need to be solved if a human trip to Mars is to be attempted. The narrated video contains 164 scenes using existing NASA footage. The video opens with approximately 30 seconds of punchy, upbeat music with quick cuts leading to the following voice overlay: "Exploration is based on intense curiosity. The desire to know what's out there. The wonder of discovery ... the fascination of finding something new that no one else has found before." The video concludes by stating the challenge that awaits the student:

> Your challenge is to think of different kinds of problems that would have to be solved in order to travel to Mars and back home again. This video contains many clues. Every image has a meaning, and some images have many meanings. Explore, discover, and find something new.

The images and narration were designed to prime the students to think about the key problems involved in the challenge of going to Mars and returning safely to Earth. The narration specifically challenges students to pose problems within the domain of planning a mission, but is not so specific that it inhibits problems that students might want to pose. Watching the *Mission to Mars* video suggests the wide variety of factors involved in planning and carrying out a mission to Mars.

Generating Research Questions. The problem-generation activity typically takes place over a period of three 50-minute classes or can be completed as a morning/afternoon activity. During the first period, the students view the video as a class and then individually pose as many problems as they can. The students then break up into small groups that take turns reviewing the video and posing additional problems upon seeing the video for the second time. Each group then synthesizes related problems to create a set of problems for the group. During the second period, each group sorts its problems into self-specified categories. Then the class categorizes all of the individual sets of problems into a master set of categories. During the final period, the class regroups around the master categories according to individual preference. Every attempt is made to give students their first choice, but we find that having the students list their top three choices is more practical. Students in each of the groups then use these problems to set a priority list of problems to solve during the entire Mission to Mars unit.

List of Questions Generated. Table 4.1 shows a list of typical questions that middle school children have asked in the past during the problem generation phase of the Mission to Mars unit. While your own students may pose other problems, we believe this list gives a good representation of what to expect.

Table 4.1

Sample Student-Generated Questions

Category	Typical student-generated questions
Onboard Resources (Supply Officers)	1. How much water will we need? 2. How much food will we need? 3. Will we need special food? 4. How much air/oxygen will we need? 5. How long will we stay? 6. How often can we do laundry? 7. What are basic nutritional needs?
Spacecraft Environment (Environmental Preservation Team)	1. Can we recycle the water we use? 2. Can we reuse the oxygen we use? 3. How will we go to the bathroom? 4. What kind of equipment will we need to take?
Navigation and Propulsion (Engineering)	1. How long will we be in space? 2. What's the distance from Earth to Mars? 3. How will we get to Mars and back? 4. How much fuel will it take? 5. How long will we stay on Mars? 6. How far is the asteroid belt from Mars? 7. What are the hazards? Can we make the trip safer? 8. Is there more than one way to get there?
Human Factors (Medical Team)	1. Will the astronauts get along? 2. How many males and females should go? 3. Will we allow the astronauts to reproduce? 4. How do you go to the bathroom in space? 5. Do we have to be a specific height and weight? 6. Will we need to exercise? 7. How often will we communicate with Earth? 8. Are there diseases we can get on Mars? 9. What if someone gets real sick or dies?
Surface Exploration (Away Team)	1. What will we use for shelter on Mars? 2. Will there be some sort of life on Mars? 3. How will we deal with the cold weather on Mars? 4. Can we start a fire on Mars? 5. Where should we land on Mars? 6. Can we get oxygen to breathe from the surface of Mars? 7. Can we get water from Mars? 8. Does Mars have seasons?

(Table continues on next page)

Table 4.1 (Continued)

Sample Student-Generated Questions

Category	Typical student-generated questions
Spacecraft Design	1. What size ship do we need? 2. How much would the ship cost? 3. Will the ship survive the long trip? 4. Can the ship survive the asteroid belt? 5. Where will we sleep, eat, work, go to the bathroom? 6. How many pounds of stuff can we take? 7. Will we have enough fuel? 8. Should we take more than one ship?

Categories and Rationale. We have produced six categories of questions that have been used successfully during implementation. At times it may be difficult to put a specific question within a specific category, and there may be some overlap. For example, should "How much water will we need" be listed under "Onboard Resources" or "Human Factors"? Certainly, some questions will cause categorization problems, while others will be clearly delineated. "Will the spacecraft survive the long and possibly dangerous trip?" is clearly a Spacecraft Design question. A description of each category is provided below.

1. *Onboard Resources*: Commonly referred to as the Supply Officers, this group is responsible for the quantity of resources the astronauts will need during the mission.
2. *Environmental Preservation*: The primary purpose of this group is to ensure the environmental health of the spacecraft. The cabin must be essentially a "mini-Earth" with proper levels of nitrogen, oxygen, and carbon dioxide balanced and filtered.
3. *Navigation & Propulsion*: Deciding which path to take to Mars is a complex task, and many variables must be taken into consideration. This group acts very much like the engineers of the team.
4. *Human Factors*: What effects will long-term space flight have on our crew? This group is primarily responsible for the physical and psychological health of the astronaut. The members of this group have a large amount of research to accomplish.
5. *Surface Exploration*: The primary goal of the mission is to explore the planet Mars. Where should the landing be? What time of year should the landing occur? Are there places on Earth where training could take place to simulate conditions at the landing site on Mars?

6. *Spacecraft Design*: What type of spacecraft will be needed for a successful trip to Mars? How much recreational room should there be? Students may find analogous situations with submarine design.

After this launching event, students are organized into different research groups to engage in extended investigations of the questions they helped generate.

STEP 6: CREATING BENCHMARK AND INVESTIGATION LESSON PLANS

Benchmark Lessons

As discussed in Chapter 3, benchmark lessons involve instances where the teacher provides instruction on disciplinary STEM concepts that have become important for students' ability to continue to pursue Project questions (see diSessa & Minstrell, 1998). Such lessons can happen when the class becomes "stuck" on a particular concept and needs instruction from the teacher to move forward, or it can happen when the teacher knows from experience that students historically tend to need assistance on particular concepts when they reach a certain point in the Project. For example, when doing a Project about a mission to Mars, a point may come in the Project when students need to understand planetary motion to move forward, or they need to understand the speed of falling objects to continue their investigations.

The teacher must take into account four important considerations when creating benchmark lessons:

1. What STEM disciplinary concepts must students understand in order to answer the project's driving question?
2. What prior misconceptions or gaps in this knowledge might students have?
3. When is the best moment to communicate this knowledge to the students?
4. In what format should this knowledge be communicated?

With respect to the first consideration about what concepts students must know to answer the driving question, the teacher should start by reviewing the standards that they mapped to the Project, the Project's concept map, and the artifacts or products students must produce and any accompanying rubrics. Next, the teacher should take into account the second consideration, what prior misconceptions or gaps students might currently hold with respect to this knowledge base. Based on this information, the teacher should choose several different conceptual areas to be the focus of benchmark lessons throughout the Project. For example, a math Project involving art and motion geometry might have a benchmark lesson about algebraic processes that enact translations and reflections and another benchmark lesson plan about algebraic processes relating to rotation. If the teacher knows that students have informal understandings of slides, flips, and turns, but also knows that students do not yet know how to map these informal understandings to symbolic notations, a benchmark lesson plan would be an excellent place to make these connections. However, the teacher might not always anticipate the topics students will need a benchmark lesson on, particularly if it is their first time trying a Project. The teacher should be ready to add benchmark lessons "on the fly" if the need for them arises.

Once the teacher has decided what needs to be taught and divided these concepts up into a discrete number of lessons, the next consideration is when to position these lessons in the Project sequence. Benchmark lessons are ideally situated when the teacher can create a "time for telling" (Schwartz & Bransford, 1998) and respond to an immediate need that has arisen while students have been pursuing their Project work. In other words, students should be allowed to progress in their investigations until a moment has come where a "need to know" has been created and the students are positioned to understand exactly why and for what purpose they need to learn the STEM disciplinary concepts. For example, in a Project involving designing an energy efficient tiny house, a moment might come in the Project when elementary students realize they need to be able to take the area of irregular shapes. The teacher anticipates this as a potential gap in their understanding, as the class has only in the past covered how to take the area of canonical shapes (e.g., a square or a rectangle). The teacher might position a benchmark lesson on the area of irregular shapes to occur during the Project sequence right when students will need that knowledge.

The final consideration the teacher must make when designing benchmark lesson plans is how to organize students' learning. We typically structure benchmark lessons using the 5-E format, even though they tend to involve more teacher guidance than other more prototypical 5-E lessons. The 5-E structure does leave space for the teacher to directly communicate content information. Specifically, during the Explain phase of a 5-E lesson, students explain in their own words what they discovered from their mini-investigations during the Explore phase of the lesson. After eliciting student explanations, the teacher can bring all of their informal ideas and understandings together, introducing terminology, algorithms, and processes for students to use. The students can experiment with adopting these during the Elaborate portion of the lesson, and the teacher can assess their new understandings in the final Evaluate phase. Introducing needed disciplinary STEM concepts after a round of student exploration and discussion, rather than before, gives students an opportunity to deeply understand where these concepts come from and connect them to their prior knowledge. Choosing carefully when a benchmark lesson occurs will allow the students to immediately see how disciplinary, sometimes abstract, concepts tie in to answering a complex, applied STEM problem.

Investigation Lessons

Investigation lessons serve a slightly different purpose than benchmark lessons; they serve to deepen students' disciplinary knowledge, help students to understand how this knowledge can be applied to certain Project tasks, and allow students to make progress on their Project goals in a more structured manner. We also recommend the 5-E format for investigation lesson plans, but the considerations for teachers are slightly different. The teacher should consider these questions:

1. What key STEM concepts are at the heart of this project and what are the "big ideas" I want students to walk away with?
2. What is the best way to give students ownership of these big ideas?
3. How can I support students in seeing how these ideas arise in their group's specific work and in the work of all the groups working on this project?

With respect to the first consideration, the teacher should look critically at the Project concepts and think about what the most important, compelling STEM ideas are that both connect to the heart of the Project's purpose and the desired learning outcomes for the Project. The teacher should strategically choose topics for investigative lessons that would give students deeper insight into and understanding of these ideas. Investigative lessons can also serve to teach students more generally the processes for scientific inquiry they may need to complete a Project's activity. For example, investigative lessons could cover topics like using simulation software to make observations and answer questions or using graphing programs to engage in mathematical exploration.

The second consideration is how teachers can best facilitate students' ownership of the big ideas at the heart of the Project. This usually involves some sort of guided discovery where, within the 5-E lesson format, students come to understand the disciplinary ideas on their own terms and then engage in significant discussion and refinement of their ideas and observations. Students should have the opportunity to continually reflect on and revise their thinking and any products they are creating through these mini-investigations. Students also will need a lot of support and scaffolding, particularly if the concepts they are exploring are less familiar to them. The resources that can be given for support, as well as the kind of feedback the learners will receive, are especially important during more open-ended investigations.

The final consideration is how the teacher can support students in seeing how the ideas from the investigation relate to their group's Project and the Projects of others. Investigative lessons may involve students working on the product they are creating for the Project in a structured way (e.g., everyone uses simulation software to test the initial design for their balsa wood bridges). It also may involve activities that are slightly more disconnected from the actual Project activities (e.g., the students evaluating the tension and compression forces acting upon a given set of bridges, in preparation to design their own bridge). In the former case, it is important that the teacher supports students in seeing not only how the lesson applies to their Project but also how the disciplinary concepts arise in different ways in other groups' work. This can be done through class discussions or intergroup collaboration. In the latter case, it is important that the teacher makes clear connections to the Project work.

STEP 7: PLANNING FOR FORMATIVE AND SUMMATIVE ASSESSMENT DURING THE PROJECT

Two final aspects of a Project that a teacher must plan for are how to formatively assess student progress and how to summatively assess students (usually through a culminating artifact or product). To foster *understanding* rather than just *doing*, formative assessment guides teachers and learners to reflect meaningfully on their activities and progress towards achieving some goal. Formative assessment is defined as any act of assessment undertaken during the learning process to inform the learner as she moves from a current level of ability toward the mastery of some intended learning outcome (Brookhart, 2017). Formative assessment is often defined with relation to diagnostic assessment (assessment given before teaching has occurred to identify prior knowledge or conceptions) and summative assessment (assessment given after the conclusion of teaching on a topic to evaluate student learning). Barron et al. (1998) noted,

> Most projects that we have observed in classrooms involve no explicit formative assessment. As a result, it is not clear to the teachers what is and

what is not being learned, and it is not clear how to adapt their instruction accordingly. (p. 284)

While the benefits of formative assessment are deeply important to the goals of PBI, several key barriers in implementation exist, including (a) assessing for rote learning or memorization rather than conceptual knowledge, (b) little collaboration among teachers when selecting or designing assessment tools, (c) overemphasis on grading, and (d) emphasis on ranking or competition between students rather than assessment against criterion (Black & Wiliam, 1998). For these reasons, when planning their formative assessments for Project units, teachers should seek to critically consider how well their assessments capture different levels of understanding—ranging from a basic knowledge of STEM-related terms and algorithms to a deeper knowledge of STEM processes, relationships, and "big ideas."

In addition, teachers should collaborate with other teachers in their department or cross-departmentally when designing assessments. For example, if an assessment is a written report, a science teacher implementing the project might collaborate with the English language arts teacher. If an assessment involves the analysis of collected data, the science teacher implementing the project might collaborate with a math teacher. Finally, the teacher must carefully consider the emphasis of "the grade" the student receives and how to ensure that grades are criterion-based such that all students can have the potential to reach mastery. By jointly defining learning appropriate goals and developing driving questions aligned to these goals, teachers and learners can evaluate progress against specific criteria developed from the goals or driving question. This supports teaching and learning which avoids using assessments to rank students or foster competition between students. For example, a driving question developed by Petrosino (1998) allowed students to explore how specific variables (rocket texture, number of fins, and cone shape) in rocket design determine the height of a rocket launch. The structure of this driving question lent itself to evaluate students against three criteria (abilities to engage in scientific inquiry, statistical reasoning, and physical reasoning) rather than ranking students against each other.

The social organization and collaboration that are often inherent in PBI have interesting implications for formative assessment. The high degree of collaboration may require assessment of the small group rather than the individual, a departure from how typical assessments are used in the classroom. Furthermore, having many groups in a classroom working towards similar goals can produce differences among the topics that students are focused on. This "distributed expertise" requires assessing where student groups are against the learning goal their group is pursuing, rather than a common learning goal for the entire class. For example, students exploring rocket design may take up different variables of interest, requiring assessment that provides feedback on their specific interests.

Often defined by the driving question, the final product of a Project-based unit is any type of collaboratively constructed representation of student learning. This can typically function as a form of summative assessment if the learning ends here or as a formative assessment if students are allowed to evaluate their artifact and re-engage in inquiry to iteratively refine their creation. For example, learners test rockets by evaluating the shape of the rocket cone and determine that curved cones produce higher flight paths than pointed cones. The teacher could use students' final rocket designs and data as a summative assessment of their abilities to discuss the physics of flight or allow their designs to exist as a formative assessment for which students can determine new questions about cone shape to ask and answer. When designing a summative assessment, the teacher should consider the characteristics of the final product that they wish to use to evaluate students. The teacher can create a grading rubric to capture these characteristics or collaboratively codevelop this rubric with students.

While the creation of the final artifact is often related to the driving question and indicative of the end goal of the learning unit, punctuated formative assessments can help focus the teacher and learners by scaffolding progress towards the goal. For example, students studying rocket design were required to submit paper designs of their rockets and plan for assessing the individual design elements. This type of scaffolding allows the teacher to determine if the class needs to engage in some form of direct-teach or lecture surrounding a certain topic to aid in their progress towards the final goal. Thus, teachers should try to carefully align their formative and summative assessments during the planning phase.

The use of a real or simulated professional audience in a Project allows formative assessment to occur through dialogue between the student-learners and the professional. For example, students working with rocket design can evaluate their designs with a professional aerospace engineer before launching to test their initial conjectures with a knowledgeable other. A professional audience can also provide a formal evaluation of the Project product in a way that serves as an external summative assessment. During the planning phase, the teacher should carefully consider at what point(s) in the project a professional audience will be brought in and how their presence will support formative or summative assessment.

A final issue to discuss is the role of technology in assessment. A review of technology used in project-based learning studies, revealed that the most popular technology integrated with project-based learning was social media, followed by cloud computing, computer modeling, learning management systems, and finally websites (Rahmawati et al., 2020). The teacher's ability to give guidance during the learning process is the most influential factor for the success of technology integration in project-based learning. Clearly, an alignment between technology and teachers are required to attain a successful integration of technology in the learning and assessment process.

The teacher's ability in guiding the assessment process with technology integration is the most influential factor for the success of technology integration in PBI. When this is coupled with students' ability in communication, learning framework, students' self-efficacy, students' need and interests, prior experience regarding technology has shown assessment is effectively and seamlessly integrated into our designed units.

The emergence of more affordable technology, particularly the increase in one-to-one computing environments, has the potential to radically transform Project-based classrooms and the assessment in these learning environments. Formative assessments can now more easily be created by teachers, shared among teaching peers, delivered to students, and automatically graded. This shortens the feedback cycle of formative assessments and allows for learners to instantly receive meaningful guidance on their progress towards answering a driving question or pursuing a learning appropriate goal. Furthermore, computer-delivered and automatically graded formative assessments can occur more frequently with less time devoted to each assessment, potentially normalizing the process of assessment and feedback and perhaps decreasing the notion of assessments as a tool for ranking students. These kinds of formative assessments that closely track students' understanding of a variety of disciplinary ideas can be used to individualize feedback.

Technology can also connect learners with knowledgeable others or peers who can give feedback or provide guidance to support Project work through online forums, video calls, etc. Technology can provide new means of dissemination and formative assessment. For example, the product of a Project could be a website or blog post. The emergence of agent-based modeling using programming languages, such as NetLogo Web (Wilensky, 1998), also opens PBI to temporally and spatially large or small phenomena. Learners can program agents in models to behave based on prior knowledge or learning experiences and tinker with phenomena that have previously been too cumbersome to achieve in classrooms through Project-based methods. In response, students' creations, modifications, or interactions with models can be captured as data points to inform teaching and learning in STEM fields, a useful type of formative assessment.

REFERENCES

Barron, B. J., Schwartz, D. L., Vye, N. J., Moore, A., Petrosino, A., Zech, L., & Bransford, J. D. (1998). Doing with understanding: Lessons from research on problem- and project-based learning. *Journal of the Learning Sciences, 7*(3–4), 271–311.

Barron, B., Vye, N. J., Zech, L., Schwartz, D., Bransford, J. D., Goldman, S. R., Pellegrino, J., Morris, J., Garrison, S., & Kantor, R. (1995). Creating contexts for community-based problem solving: The Jasper challenge series. In C. N. Hedley, P. Antonacci, & M. Rabinowitz (Eds.), *Thinking and literacy: The mind at work* (pp. 47–71). Erlbaum.

Bernacki, M. L., & Walkington, C. (2018). The role of situational interest in personalized learning. *Journal of Educational Psychology, 110*(6), 864–881.

Black, P., & Wiliam, D. (1998). Assessment and classroom learning. *Assessment in Education: Principles, Policy & Practice, 5*(1), 7–74.

Blumenfeld, P. C., Krajcik, J. S., Kam, R., Kempler, T. M., & Geier, R. (2005, April). *Opportunity to learn in PBL for middle school science: Predicting urban student achievement and motivation* [Paper presentation]. Annual Meeting of the American Association for Research in Education, Montreal, Quebec, Canada.

Blumenfeld, P. C., Soloway, E., Marx, R. W., Krajcik, J. S., Guzdial, M., & Palincsar, A. (1991). Motivating project-based learning: Sustaining the doing, supporting the learning. *Educational Psychologist, 26*(3–4), 369–398.

Bransford, J. D., Brown, A. L., & Cocking, R. R. (2000). *How people learn: Brain, mind, experience, and school*. National Academies Press.

Brookhart, S. M. (2017). *How to give effective feedback to your students* (2nd ed.). ASCD.

Brown, A. L., & Campione, J. C. (1994). *Guided discovery in a community of learners*. MIT Press.

Center for Technology Transfer and Commercialization. (n.d.). *The adventures of Jasper Woodbury: Videodisc-based adventures that focus on mathematical problem finding and problem solving designed for students in Grades 5 and up*. https://cttc.co/technologies/adventures-jasper-woodbury-videodisc-based-adventures-focus-mathematical-problem-finding-and-problem-solving-designed-students-grades-5-and

Cognition and Technology Group at Vanderbilt. (1992). The Jasper experiment: An exploration of issues in learning and instructional design. *Educational Technology Research and Development, 40*(1), 65–80.

diSessa, A. A., & Minstrell, J. (1998). Cultivating conceptual change with benchmark lessons. In J. Minstrell, J. G. Greeno, & S. Goldman (Eds.), *Thinking practices in mathematics and science learning* (pp. 155–187). Erlbaum.

Geier, R., Blumenfeld, P. C., Marx, R. W., Krajcik, J. S., Fishman, B., Soloway, E., & Clay Chambers, J. (2008). Standardized test outcomes for students engaged in inquiry-based science curricula in the context of urban reform. *Journal of Research in Science Teaching, 45*(8), 922–939.

Graesser, A. C., Green, M. C., Strange, J. J., & Brock, T. C. (2002). *Narrative impact: Social and cognitive foundations*. Psychology Press.

Hestenes, D., & Wells, M. (1992). A mechanics baseline test. *The Physics Teacher, 30*(3), 159–166.

Hickey, D. T., Moore, A. L., & Pellegrino, J. W. (2001). The motivational and academic consequences of two innovative mathematics environments: Do curricular innovations and reforms make a difference? *American Educational Research Journal, 38*(3), 611–652.

Krajcik, J. S., & Czerniak, C. M. (2014). *Teaching science in elementary and middle school: A project-based approach*. Routledge.

Krajcik, J. S., Czerniak, C., & Berger, C. (1999). *Teaching children science: A project-based approach*. McGraw-Hill College.

Minstrell, J. (1992). Facets of students' knowledge and relevant instruction. In R. Duit, F. Goldberg, & H. Niedderer (Eds.), *Research in physics learning: Theoretical issues and empirical studies* (pp. 110–128). Kiel.

National Research Council. (2004). *Engaging school: Fostering high school students' motivation to learn*. National Academies Press.

Novak, J. D., & Cañas, A. J. (2006). *The theory underlying concept maps and how to construct them. Florida Institute for Human and Machine Cognition*. http://cmap.ihmc.us/publications/researchpapers/theorycmaps/TheoryUnderlyingConceptMaps.bck-11-01-06.htm

Petrosino, A. J. (1998). *The use of reflection and revision in hands-on experimental activities by at-risk children* [Unpublished doctoral dissertation]. Vanderbilt University.

Petrosino, A., & Koehler, M. (2007). Teachers as designers: Pre and in-service teachers' authoring of anchor video as a means to professional development. In R. Goldman, R. Pea, B. Barron, & S. J. Derry (Eds.), *Video research in the learning sciences* (pp. 411–423). Routledge.

Rahmawati, A., Suryani, N., Akhyar, M., & Sukarmin. (2020). Technology-integrated project-based learning for pre-service teacher education: A systematic literature review. *Open Engineering, 10*(1), 620–629. https://doi.org/10.1515/eng-2020-0069

Schwartz, D. L., & Bransford, J. D. (1998). A time for telling. *Cognition and Instruction, 16*(4), 475–522. https://doi.org/10.1207/s1532690xci1604_4

Sizer, T. (1984). *Horace's compromise: The dilemma of the American high school*. Houghton Mifflin Company.

Stuever, N. L. (2009). A post-modern perspective on curriculum. *Journal of Teaching and Learning, 6*(1), 87–90.

Wiggins, G., & McTighe, J. (1998). *Understanding by design*. ASCD.

Wilensky, U. (1998). *NetLogo Virus model*. http://ccl.northwestern.edu/netlogo/models/Virus

Williams, S. M. (1992). Putting case-based instruction into context: Examples from legal and medical education. *Journal of the Learning Sciences, 2*, 367–427.

Yager, R. E., & Penick, J. E. (1986). Perceptions of four age groups toward science classes, teachers, and the value of science. *Science Education, 70*(4), 355–363.

CHAPTER 5

PBI ACROSS ENGINEERING, COMPUTER SCIENCE, AND MATHEMATICS

In this chapter, we discuss issues surrounding PBI in specific disciplinary STEM fields, specifically engineering, computer science, and mathematics. Much of the established research on PBI has been in science education, and these three additional fields each have unique considerations and advancements for PBI implementation. At the end of the chapter, we are also treated to some of the leaders in the field of PBI across these STEM fields as we ask them what trends or issues they feel are critical as PBI moves forward. These profiles provide unique insight into implementation of PBI and important issues to consider across the domains of science, computer science, data literacy, engineering, and mathematics.

PBI IN ENGINEERING

Issues With Project-Based Learning Engineering Education

PBI continues to gain interest within the engineering education community (Edward, 2004; Iscioglu & Kale, 2010; Lou et al., 2011; Palmer & Hall, 2011). This continued interest is attributed to PBI's ability to foster professional skills valued in engineering graduates such as communication, teamwork, and critical thinking (Prince & Felder, 2006; Woodcock et al., 2019). In K–12 educational contexts, the importance of PBI is echoed

---

Frameworks for Integrated Project-Based Instruction in STEM Disciplines, pp. 111–131
Copyright © 2024 by Information Age Publishing
www.infoagepub.com

in national reports and standards. Specifically, the Next Generation Science Standards (NGSS) have reiterated a commitment to integration of science education in engineering and engineering design at all levels of schooling, providing a critical avenue for PBI to serve as a platform for facilitating such integration into the curriculum. Furthermore, engineering projects providing K–12 students with opportunities to address major contemporary societal problems (e.g., global environmental change, energy sufficiency, and providing clean water and food) are instrumental in inspiring students to pursue STEM education and careers by exposing them to a variety of real-world applications of STEM content (National Research Council, 2012).

However, in spite of abundantly cited benefits of PBI (e.g., Krajcik & Shin, 2022; Miller & Krajcik, 2019; Woods & Walkington, 2020), student response has not always been positive. Studies have noted that students find PBI overwhelming, which culminates in student discomfort and suboptimal engagement (Savage et al., 2007; Yadav et al., 2011). These findings are in line with broader research on student negative response to nontraditional teaching methods in STEM fields (Borrego et al., 2018; Finelli et al., 2018; Shekhar & Borrego, 2017a, 2017b; Shekhar et al., 2020; Tharayil et al., 2018). Although this research has been conducted mostly in undergraduate education, K–12 education may adapt these findings to suit contexts and constraints when implementing PBI. This will facilitate translation of research on PBI vertically along the different educational levels (K–12, undergraduate, graduate) as well as horizontally across different STEM topics and contexts.

One way to approach PBI in engineering that addresses this challenge is to think about instruction around the following three-step process:

1. Instructors should optimize the complexity of the Projects by adjusting the scope of the Projects based on student feedback (Armbruster et al., 2009). This may help reduce student discomfort. Teachers can use student feedback, such as the time required for project completion, to monitor the scope of the Project.
2. Introducing ambitious and time-consuming Projects earlier in the semester or school year is another strategy that teachers may use in PBI classrooms. Researchers have noted that activities implemented near the end of the semester receive less student interest due to limited time (Wilke, 2003).
3. Teachers should make sure that students are trained and possess required background knowledge to complete the assigned Project tasks (Frank et al., 2003). This can help create an effective learning environment. The teachers may use demonstration sessions where students follow along sample problems in class

before working on their assigned Projects. Such opportunities not only help students with necessary and valuable skills, but also support further inquiry by allowing students to explore software tools or other project equipment.

PBI and the Maker Education Movement in Engineering Education

Another way to approach PBI in engineering is based on the maker movement. The maker movement is an encompassing term for designers, inventors, and tinkering enthusiasts. It includes artisans and computer programmers and lies at the intersection of engineering and computer science education. The movement has gained great popularity in the past decade and now has numerous associated websites, magazines, and conferences. Makers tap into a universal thread of self-reliance and combine that with informal learning, often building on powerful personal technology like 3-D printers. Creating projects in garages, workshops, community spaces, and bedrooms ignites the imaginations of young and old alike.

Our colleague, Dr. Rob Rouse, a former high school chemistry teacher in New York City and a founding member of Southern Methodist University's Maker Education Project, focuses on exploring the role of culture, tools, and equity in learning in the emerging field of maker education. According to Dr. Rouse, the maker movement has influenced a complementary movement in K–16 education known as the maker education movement. While sharing some similarities, these are distinct movements, as the maker movement occurs in informal, unsupervised spaces. These makerspaces often are not friendly places for young people to hang out and do work. They are almost exclusively geared towards adults and professionals. The *maker education movement* is the term that we use to describe when teachers, administrators, or researchers take up concrete and abstract concepts valued by the maker movement and implement them in educational settings to help promote students learning a variety of content disciplines (e.g., science, math) or demonstrating particular skills (e.g., collaboration, creativity, resilience). For this reason, the maker education movement is very different from the maker movement.

Despite significant differences between the maker movement and the maker education movement, one commonality is the venue in which the action happens—the makerspace. School-based makerspaces can look very different. Some are set up in classrooms, some are unique spaces, some are in art classrooms, and some are in the school library. Many school-based makerspaces are underconceptualized, understaffed, and academically ill-defined due to lack of formal training, financial resources, and curriculum and assessments (Blikstein, 2018). Yet a school-based makerspace being academically ill defined could be an advantage. In an innovative school, educators can use the makerspace in innovative and creative ways, as an asset. At a less innovative school, educators might struggle to find ways to meaningfully use the makerspace, creating a burden.

Currently, makerspaces are popular and have been propelled by a more general focus on STEM education that has taken place—so many schools have them or want them. The challenge is that very few schools seem to know why they want them or how they will use them to complement the school's mission or values. Administrators and teachers may believe that a makerspace will be a panacea for STEM instruction in the school. This view of school-based makerspace instruction is unpopular with researchers of the maker education movement (Godhe et al., 2019; Martin, 2015).

Given the state of makerspace instruction in schools, most schools where educators struggle to use makerspaces to their full potential could use PBI to give their makerspaces more purpose. Makerspace instruction and PBI share many similarities:

1. Both are rooted in constructivist and constructionist learning theory.
2. Both promote active and student-centered learning environments.
3. Both emphasize collaboration, problem-solving, learning from one's mistakes, and persevering through failures.
4. Both encourage students to connect to their lived experience and do work related to personally meaningful topics.
5. Both promote interdisciplinarity.
6. Finally, they both have the potential to emphasize content and skills.

The influence is not only in one direction. Makerspaces have the potential to complement PBI. A well-equipped makerspace could serve as a place to prototype potential solutions in a Project. The types of high-resolution prototypes that can be created in a makerspace would be excellent for displaying publicly to real-life audiences—a trademark of PBI. PBI may help a makerspace as well. Many school-based makerspace projects are short and yield ephemeral products. Yet, makerspaces outside of school typically involve intricate projects built with care to last. Blending PBI with makerspace instruction could yield products that are more substantial and establish the makerspace as a valuable tool.

Additionally, perhaps the biggest threat to the maker education movement is an emphasis on "doing" at the expense of "doing with understanding" (Barron et al., 1998). Conversely, doing with reflection and revision has become well established with strong theoretical implementations of PBI, which could benefit makerspaces. Makerspaces are often associated with design. There are interesting opportunities to connect makerspace instruction with human-centered design or design thinking. The methods and mindsets that come with practicing human-centered design and design thinking, including empathy, could mesh well with PBI.

PBI IN COMPUTER SCIENCE

What Does PBI in Computer Science Incorporate?

In prior sections of this book, we have mainly focused on PBI in the context of math, science, and engineering education. However, there is increasing attention on the importance of topics like computational thinking, data science, and programming in integrated STEM education. Thus, specifically considering the role of PBI in computer science education is important. Indeed, STEM fields are rapidly integrating their practices with those of computer science.

The report by the Committee on STEM Education of the National Science and Technology Council (2018) entitled *Charting A Course For Success: America's Strategy for STEM Education* emphasized the critical importance of engaging students where disciplines converge. In other words, to make STEM learning more meaningful and inspiring to students, instruction should focus on complex real-world problems and challenges that require initiative and creativity. Engaging learners in integrated disciplinary activities such as PBI (as well as science fairs and robotics clubs) requires students to identify and solve problems using knowledge, skills, and methods from multiple disciplines. Another objective, according to the report, is teaching learners to tackle problems using multiple disciplines, such as learning data science by combining basic mathematics, statistics, and computer science to study a societal problem. Such activities help to create a STEM-literate population and prepare Americans for the rapidly evolving workplace.

Another key finding of the Committee on STEM Education of the National Science and Technology Council (2018) report was the need to build computational literacy. This finding recognizes the role that digital literacy has in empowering people with the tools to find information, answer questions, and share ideas responsibly and safely. Computational thinking is a critical skill for today's world. Computational thinking, which includes computer science, is not just about using computing devices effectively but also how to solve complex real-world problems with data, a skill that can be learned at an early age via PBI. The report concluded with the acknowledgment that these tools have the potential to advance equity in formal educational settings and to offer rapid reskilling or upskilling opportunities in the workplace.

Zilberman and Ice (2021) explained that STEM occupations are projected to grow over twice as fast as the total for all occupations in the next decade. They explained the U.S. Bureau of Labor Statistics 2019–2029 employment projections showed that occupations in STEM fields are expected to grow 8% by 2029, compared with 3.7% for all occupations. While this is encouraging for STEM fields, Zilberman and Ice noted specifically that high demand for computer occupations is largely the reason for the expected increase in STEM employment in the next decade. Therefore, the future of PBI in STEM education will involve providing opportunities for students to use computational methods to engage in traditional disciplinary practices. To support this, education researchers have developed a taxonomy of computational practices to support STEM disciplinary learning, divided into four branches (Weintrop et al., 2016):

- Data practices,
- Modeling and simulation practices,
- Computational problem-solving practices, and
- Systems thinking practices.

More can be read about each of these computational practice branches in the Weintrop et al. (2016) article. However, supporting secondary learners in engagement with these practices throughout PBI necessitates providing that same support for preservice STEM teachers in teacher preparation programs. For example, our work with secondary STEM preservice teachers has involved using computational simulations to explore complex systems such as ecosystems, viral epidemics, and social phenomena like residential segregation. By exploring complex phenomena with computational simulations, teachers learn about complex phenomena through data collection, programming, and systems thinking.

An exciting area we see with PBI and computer science is current work by our colleagues Deborah Fields and Yasmin Kafai. They discuss the notion of "hard fun" as the idea that learners actually enjoy or have fun when making complex or "hard" things. In the process, students can develop deep understanding about subject matter and about themselves as learners. Original work in this area was by Seymour Papert (1980), who viewed learning as the process of designing and creating things (artifacts—digital or physical) of personal and social importance and in the process connecting old and new knowledge as well as interacting with others in social spaces. Fields and Kafai (2020) described hard fun in the area of programming with Scratch (https://scratch.mit.edu) and electronic textiles; they presented six pedagogical principles for practically applying PBI in personally relevant ways that engage deep learning in the classroom: (a) promoting creativity within constraints, (b) growing complexity in a series of projects, (c) starting with aesthetics first, (d) celebrating mistakes, (e) keeping track of progress, and (f) reflecting as computational communication. Success stories of the Scratch platform and community as well as the maker movement have demonstrated that millions of students can be encouraged to be programmers and to make electronics in classrooms, afterschool programs, and informal and online spaces (Fields & Kafai, 2020). In short, they asserted that learning through making can be hard fun and yield high levels of rewards, but only when making the things (or programming) is a challenge to the creators and when the creators are educationally and socially supported during the process.

UTeach Computer Science Principles Curriculum and Instruction

Dr. Petrosino has worked with the UTeach Program at the University of Texas at Austin since its inception. The UTeach program works to certify secondary STEM teachers by recruiting and training undergraduate and postgraduate STEM degree pursuing individuals. The penultimate course in the UTeach program, Project-Based Instruction, trains preservice teachers in the theoretical and practical aspects of planning and executing projects within their subject area of interest. One initiative involving UTeach that is especially exciting is a partnership between UTeach and the New York City Public Schools. This collaboration establishes a research-practice partnership (RPP) across six New York City public school districts to examine the degree to which codesign of project-based curriculum, project-based practices, and teacher supports can build organizational capacity to support the implementation of equitable computer science teaching and learning (see Petrosino et al., 2022; Petrosino et al., 2023).

This research-practice partnership team of New York City public school administrators and classroom teachers is collaborating with researchers, curriculum developers, and professional learning and support specialists to identify (a) effective organizational conditions and supports, (b) PBI approaches, (c) noncognitive approaches, and (d) accompanying teacher supports and student and teacher materials that improve Black and Latino/a student participation, learning, and engagement in computer science. Methodologically, a design-based implementation research approach is used. This project addresses three overarching research questions:

1. What organizational conditions, processes, and supports are associated with improved participation by Black and Latino/a

students in computer science, as measured by the diversity of students enrolling in computer science courses?
2. What kinds of PBI strategies, materials, and interventions are associated with improved student learning in UTeach Computer Science Principles among Black and Latino/a students, as measured by student scores on projects according to standard project rubrics and unit and Advanced Placement exam scores?
3. What kinds of noncognitive approaches (e.g., teacher messaging, classroom routines, recruitment strategies, etc.) are associated with improved engagement and motivation by Black and Latino/a students in UTeach Computer Science Principles and retention in computer science based on enrollment in following computer science courses?

Over the past decade, occupations in STEM have grown at a rate twice that of non-STEM occupations in the U.S., with computing jobs making up nearly half of all STEM employment (Fayer et al., 2017). This trend is expected to continue, as STEM occupations are projected to grow at a yearly rate of 8%—double the rate projected for all other occupations—through 2029 (Zilberman & Ice, 2021). A diverse STEM talent pool is critical to realize the national potential to be a global leader in innovation and advancement in STEM fields. In 2013, the U.S. Department of Commerce found that only 7% of computing positions were held by African Americans, and 6% were held by Latino/as (Landivar, 2013). These imbalances ensure limitations to innovation. In 2017, female participation in Advanced Placement computer science was 23.5%; only 3.74% of test takers were Black, and 11.69% were Latino/a (Ericson, 2018).

By focusing on Black and Latino/a students—both historically underrepresented groups in STEM and computer science nationally (Calabrese Barton & Tan, 2018) and in computer science in New York State and New York City in particular—we aim to identify classroom-based strategies for broadening participation in computer science by improving engagement and achievement for these two populations (Milesi et al., 2017). We recognize the many classroom variables influencing the trajectories of underrepresented students in STEM, including strategies to develop interest and confidence in STEM, availability of academic supports, access to STEM resources, and opportunities to access and build STEM social capital.

In addition to strengthening student-centered instructional approaches that engage learners in solving problems relevant to their community (Marshall & Alston, 2014), particular attention is paid to directly address stereotype threat with students, acknowledging student identity in the classroom (Steele & Cohn-Vargas, 2013), providing successful examples of underserved groups in STEM, and affirming student values (Cohen & Sherman, 2014). The UTeach Computer Science Principles curriculum and instruction is strengthened to explicitly address culturally responsive pedagogies (Wlodkowski & Ginsberg, 1995) that encourage Black and Latino/a student participation in computer science.

A primary goal of the project is to use what we learn through the development and testing of various approaches and interventions to expand, refine, and differentiate the UTeach Computer Science Principles curriculum and accompanying teacher support materials, professional learning, and implementation support model. We anticipate a need to expand the curriculum and teacher materials to include differentiated content for students working at different levels, for example. We may add noncognitive scaffolds to the curriculum (e.g., growth mindset activities to bolster self-efficacy; Yeager et al., 2019) and noncognitive interventions, such as teacher messaging or routines that promote inclusion and build student confidence and a sense of belonging. Another high priority is expanding teacher support materials to promote development of not only curricular and content understanding, but also pedagogical content knowledge, specifically with regard to project-based learning. Such educative teacher materials (Davis & Krajcik, 2005) might include expository text, narrative or multimedia classroom examples, and rationales for specific instructional recommendations.

To build organizational capacity to successfully implement equitable computer science teaching and learning, a necessary focus of this project is to glean insights into the district and school structures, processes, tools, and supports that either support or impede progress. In particular, we focus on the many organizational variables that influence the trajectories of underrepresented students in STEM, including opportunities and expectations to take STEM courses, availability of academic supports, access to STEM material resources, fostering parental support, and opportunities to access and build STEM social capital.

PBI IN MATHEMATICS

Over the past decade, the first author had the privilege of working with pre- and in-service teachers in the UTeach Program at the University of Texas at Austin in a variety of school districts in the Austin Metropolitan Area to learn about, plan, and execute Projects. One partner school, Manor New Tech High School in Manor, Texas, has transitioned to fully integrating the collaborative, PBI model for all students and academic subjects. It has been wonderful to see how successful PBI can be in addressing the improving the learning outcomes of students. However, the success has largely been experienced in science and humanities courses. Mathematics has not yet seemed to fit in with the collaborative PBI approach. Similarly, within the UTeach Program, we have struggled to help math majors and math educators see the value of PBI. However, we discuss two cases that demonstrate the synchronicity between mathematics and project-based methods (or similar collaborative pedagogies): the Jasper Woodbury Problem-Solving Series and Jo Boaler's work with mathematics instruction and school reform.

Case 1: The Jasper Woodbury Problem-Solving Series

One early attempt at bridging the gap between collaborative PBI and mathematics is the Jasper Woodbury Problem-Solving Series developed at Vanderbilt University (Cognition and Technology Group at Vanderbilt, 1992). The Jasper Woodbury Problem-Solving Series is an example of a video-based instructional macro context for complex problem generation and problem-solving. A typical classroom using this resource would begin by engaging with a mathematically rich video posing problems in a video-based narrative. Students work collaboratively to identify and define problems within the narrative and use information from the video to engage in mathematical exploration and generate a solution. The theoretical framework underlying the series includes (a) a constructivist and Deweyan-oriented philosophy of the purpose of learning, (b) a cognitive-science-informed view of the nature of learning, and (c) a commitment to using generative activities and cooperative learning situations. The Jasper series affords mathematical activities in a way that traditional mathematics problem-solving materials do not. However, whether these features are utilized depends on the teaching model at work in the classroom and in the greater schooling context.

One of the largest studies on anchored instruction involved a field implementation of four anchor videos from *The Adventures of Jasper Woodbury* (Hickey et al., 2001). These anchors were used over the course of a school year by teachers in 17 classes in seven states in the southeastern United States. In the majority of the classes, the Jasper instruction took the place of the students' regular mathematics instruction. Ten comparison classes were matched on key demographic variables, including socioeconomic status, location, gender, race/ethnicity, and mathematical achievement. All students were administered a series of tests at the beginning and end of the school year. One test examined students' skills solving word problems. Although Jasper students had not received additional practice on written word problems, they performed significantly better than comparison students at the end of the school year. Jasper students were able to transfer the skills they had acquired in the context of solving Jasper problems to written word problems.

Students took a series of tests designed to assess their abilities to define and formulate problems. They were given complex story problems in written form and were asked to identify goals that would need to be addressed to solve these problems. They were also shown mathematical formulations and asked to identify the goal that each formula would satisfy. These aspects of problem-solving are unique to the Jasper anchors and are not part of traditional problem-solving instruction. As expected, Jasper students performed better than comparison students on the posttest.

Finally, self-report measures of students' attitudes were collected. Jasper students showed more positive change relative to comparison students in five areas: (a) a reduction in mathematics anxiety, (b) an increase in their beliefs about their ability to perform successfully in mathematics, (c) greater interest in mathematics, (d) greater interest in solving complex problems, and (e) opinions that mathematics was more useful in solving problems from everyday life. The Jasper Woodbury Problem-Solving Series shares the central tenets of situated inquiry, use of learning technologies, collaborative design, and generative structure. The Jasper Woodbury Problem-Solving Series provides strong evidence that these tenets are productive for the design of mathematics learning environments (Cognition and Technology Group at Vanderbilt, 1997). Around the same time period that the Jasper Project was winding down from its original research, other researchers in the field began exploring the relationship between PBI and mathematics instruction.

Case 2: School-Based Mathematics Reform

One important approach to mathematics and PBI is a model of math education that Boaler (2002) presented in her book *Experiencing School Mathematics* as well as in much of her subsequent work (Boaler, 2015, 2016). Boaler presented findings from a 3-year case study describing two schools that implemented a variety of novel mathematics teaching practices with hundreds of students. Boaler collected assessments, surveys, observations, and interviews to show the ways various approaches to mathematics teaching influenced students' understanding and beliefs. One school used a traditional approach to mathematics, while the comparison school used an approach consistent with the fundamentals of PBI. Boaler provided evidence of (a) the ways in which "traditional" and "reform-oriented" mathematics teaching approaches can impact student attitude, beliefs, and achievement; (b) the impact of tracking and heterogeneous ability grouping; (c) the effectiveness of different teaching methods in preparing students for the demands of the real world and the 21st century; and (d) the relationship between gender, teaching practices, and the potential for equity in mathematics education. Boaler drew new conclusions about the ways that traditional teaching methods lead to limited forms of knowledge that are ineffective in nonschool settings and detailed some of the promises of an approach consistent with PBI.

Haase (2016, para. 6) quoted Jo Boaler from her youcubed.org website (translated from the original Portuguese):

> So what is multidimensional mathematics? It is real mathematics. Let's consider the work of a mathematician: She first has to pose an important problem, then map out a mathematical approach, she will probably collaborate with others on ideas, and engage in what Lakatos describes as a zig-zagging process of conjecturing, refining counter examples and proving. She has to form a mathematical model, apply methods, draw diagrams, connect ideas, reason about connections and communicate in different forms. The work is multidimensional. When math is taught as a multidimensional subject in classrooms students engage more, enjoy math more and achieve at higher levels.

What Boaler has described is harmonious with PBI. In the Project-based mathematics classroom, students wrestle with open-ended problems and engage in a dialogic learning process. Throughout the learning experience, the students propose ideas and act as skeptics for each other. Every student has a role to ensure that all ideas are heard and challenged. The work is creative and, most importantly, gives every student a chance to develop their mathematical understandings. Students craft their ideas, blend them together, and then share them with the class. The learning experience culminates when groups of students summarize their ideas in a written format to share publicly.

Summary

These two cases exemplify the importance of conceptual mathematics learning, situated projects, and collaboration in improving mathematics education. PBI has the potential to bring together the features described in the above cases into a framework that supports teacher learning, instructional design, and student learning. In both mathematics and science classrooms, students master the language of math but in very different ways. In the science class, students are focused on using math as a tool, whereas in math class, students are engaged in the creation of the mathematics itself. This is a compelling and reachable vision that may promote Project-based math across the nation.

PROFILES OF PBI FROM ACROSS THE STEM DISCIPLINES

In this section, we contextualize the multidisciplinary and interdisciplinary nature of PBI by giving some excerpts from current leaders who work across STEM disciplines. These excerpts show current areas of focus for expanding the science of how people learn through PBI and the most pressing issues facing this field.

Victor Lee: PBI in Mathematics Education and Makerspaces

Victor Lee is an associate professor in the Graduate School of Education at Stanford University, and he sees the future of PBI as revolving around a few areas in particular. These areas include hyperlocal projects where students are actively engaged in their local community. In Denver, Colorado, relationships between schools and the city parks have kids planting trees as part of their culminating PBI activity. Dr. Lee also believes the future of PBI and the maker movement are intertwined, although he believes more work is needed to determine how much structure to give maker projects, to promote learning while also valuing student autonomy. Finally, Dr. Lee recommended researchers and teachers think about projects with curated public data sets. This area is overdue for more work and could include students looking at historical census data or local police arrest data, for example, rather than designing a data collection method and collecting measurements directly. These public datasets could be powerful tools for mathematical and statistical learning.

Michelle Wilkerson: PBI in Science Education and Data Literacy

Michelle Wilkerson is an assistant professor at the University of California, Berkeley and studies how young people learn with and about computational representations like computer simulations, data visualizations, or interactive graphics, and their relationship to data literacy. She offered the following views:

> I see those thinking deeply about project-based instruction beginning to think longitudinally about development and the interaction of norms, "big ideas," and technologies (including digital tech and epistemic tools/routines) across multiple projects or years of study. This is something researchers have been looking at for a number of years. But it seems like now that the NGSS have emerged and the instructional consequences are beginning

to settle around a core set of specific tools like C-E-R (Claim-Evidence-Reasoning), model-based reasoning, agent-based modeling, block-based tools like Scratch, data analysis tools like CODAP [Common Online Data Analysis Platform], Tuva, etc., we can start to look at connections across the ecology of these computing tools as more stable entities. From that view, "project" based instruction moves toward "projects" based instruction, or the project moves from one activity to activities that spiral and build on each other from year to year toward some common goal or theme.

Dr. Wilkerson described the Writing Data Stories curriculum, a middle school series where students explore datasets related to the environment or nutrition. Students create data stories combining their experiences with the data (Finzer & Wilkerson, 2020). Dr. Wilkerson continued,

> We might more carefully consider the role of emotion, rhetoric, and experience in science teaching and learning. Doing Writing Data Stories during a pandemic and wildfires is making it so clear to me that "just pure data" and "just pure science" isn't enough to convince people to act. But connecting those data to stories, to things that people experience and feel and care about, might give us a chance. So how can we make those connections in ways that don't use feelings and experiences in a utilitarian way but make them part and parcel of what's allowed and important in the classroom setting? This also reminds me of work like that of Lama Jaber and Megan Bang, who pointed out that emotion and ways of knowing have always been core to science, even if they're not included in traditional narratives.

Gail Dickenson: PBI in Science Education and Mathematics Education

Gail Dickenson is an associate professor of Curriculum and Instruction at Texas State University and is one of the originators of the project-based UTeach class at the University of Texas at Austin. She finds that effective implementation of PBI tends to work in smaller environments like single schools. Large districts seem to lack the stability in leadership to sustain reform over the years it needs to take hold, whereas in smaller contexts (single schools, charter districts, individual teachers) where leadership is more stable, PBI reform efforts work quite well. She is encouraged by the inclusion of engineering in the NGSS and the shift in the emphasis towards evidence-based argumentation in STEM learning contexts. She explained that with roots in engineering, PBI aligns particularly well with the NGSS. Moreover, she noted that the emphasis of PBI on communicating findings also aligns well with argument-driven inquiry. For these reasons, she is hopeful teachers and administrators will be more willing to invest in PBI in the future.

Philip Bell: PBI in Science Education

Philip Bell is a professor of Learning Sciences & Human Development, the executive director of the University of Washington Institute for Science and Math Education focused on equity-focused innovation in K–12 STEM education, and codirector of the Learning in Informal and Formal Environments (LIFE) Science of Learning Center. The following are some of Dr. Bell's thoughts on the future of PBI.

First, Dr. Bell described developing social arrangements for high-quality PBI at systems-level scale.

> I've seen amazing project-based learning approaches used in specific classrooms, sometimes at a school level, and sometimes in a distributed network of educators. I have not seen a large school system take up project-based learning successfully yet. I think there are major issues in coordinating the enabling and supportive arrangements to center the instruction on meaningful projects and with authentic experts to support and serve as an audience for the project work. My sense is that we have to develop cross-sector networks that take the design and enactment of project-based instruction at systems-level scale as a truly shared endeavor (i.e., not just the teacher's or school's responsibility).
>
> Second, Dr. Bell noted the deep centering of community expertise and interests in PBI. Commercial workforce and other credentialed arenas (e.g., universities, government agencies) tend to be the experts brought into relation to project-based learning efforts—in terms of the projects selected, the experts brought in to support, etc. We need to continue efforts to broaden what gets counted as relevant expertise and project to include those who are centered in community life near the school. Elders and other knowledge holders should be engaged as experts. Community priorities should guide projects whether or not they relate to commercial interests and related educational pathways. The National Academies of Sciences, Engineering, and Medicine (2018) *Learning Through Citizen Science* report pointed to such efforts—and highlighted how such arrangements allow for the coordination of multiple epistemologies in ways that broaden what is science and who is thought to hold science-related expertise. We need more design-based research efforts to explore in this direction.

Pursuit-based instruction is an element of PBI as well.

> I have been wanting to explore meaningful project engagements at the next level—as related to broader pursuits and endeavors. The world needs individuals and multiple project teams to learn how to engage in coordinated ways in broader pursuits of social significance (e.g., reducing fossil fuel consumption, building resilience within a climate-impacted community). Many different kinds of projects would fold into this kind of pursuit-based instructional approach—as an assemblage of specific responses doing different

work that is needed. There may be this kind of thematic coordination of project-based learning efforts out in the world. I think there are important identity-related opportunities to help students see how specific projects—and a range of such things—relate to a coordinated response to a broader pursuit that has social gravity. Our state-level climate-change science ed project (http://climetime.org) opens up a space for such pursuit-based instruction; the network engaged 7,500 teachers in professional learning last year (University of Washington, 2019). We need students to learn to see how the range of project work flows into broader pursuits being explored.

Finally, Dr. Bell described taking the sociopolitical turn seriously in instruction.

The learning sciences field is going through a sociopolitical turn in social theory and method (e.g., Esmonde & Booker, 2016). There is great promise in this transformation. From the perspective of science education, I have tried to name specific equity and justice projects that represent possible areas of research and development for the next decade or so. They are listed in Table 5.1. My team is exploring particular ones, and the broader field is exploring others. This focus could and should flow into problem-based learning implementation spaces.

Bobby Garcia: PBI in Engineering and Computer Science

Bobby Garcia is a UTeach graduate and current principal at Manor New Technology High School in Manor, Texas. Manor New Tech is a nationally recognized high school utilizing PBI. The high school is strikingly different from what is found in traditional secondary education classroom settings. Applicants are accepted through a blind lottery. As a result, the student population at Manor New Tech is diverse in all aspects, including young men and women of color. The project-based learning environment sets up an atmosphere where learning is student driven, is engaging, and meets the needs of a wide variety of academic abilities. After a 2013 visit to the school, President Barack Obama (2013) concluded, "Every day, this school is proving that every child has the potential to learn the real-world skills they need to succeed in college and beyond.... You're doing things a little differently around here than a lot of high schools, and it's working" (para. 24).

CONCLUSION

These excerpts from leaders in the field of PBI show the challenges and opportunities of this approach as we move towards imagining PBI for a new generation of learners. They emphasize issues of equity, diversity, and

Table 5.1

Proposed Equity and Justice Projects for PreK-12 Science Education

Goal	Description
Engage in culture-based pedagogies.	Support expansive learning pathways for learners through culturally responsive, sustaining, and resurgent pedagogies.
Support diverse sense-making	Build educator capacity and educational resources to leverage the diverse intellectual resources learners bring to educational environments.
Disrupt ableism	Promote a cultural model of ability by leveraging and extending beyond universal design.
Promote place-based learning & ecological caring	Support science learning in outdoor settings, and help people learn to engage in ecological caring practices in support of socioecological thriving and multispecies justice.
Center racial justice	Build capacity for counterracist pedagogies and promote critical consciousness and responses around systemic racism.
Arrange for cross-age, family, & community science learning	Dismantle the age segregation associated with settler-colonial schooling, normalize a focus on cross-age and cross-generational learning communities, leverage families as codesigners of education, and make science education accountable to community goals.
Design course sequences using a range of meaningful phenomena	Design instruction where learners routinely investigate and act upon natural phenomena that have social gravity for them, their community, and society—including justice-centered phenomena.

Note. Adapted from "Infrastructuring Teacher Learning About Equitable Science Instruction," by P. Bell, 2019, *Journal of Science Teacher Education, 30*(7), 681–690. © Taylor & Francis. Used with permission.

scale. They also noted the increasing importance of computing and data science, and the centering of community expertise.

REFERENCES

Armbruster, P., Patel, M., Johnson, E., & Weiss, M. (2009). Active learning and student-centered pedagogy improve student attitudes and performance in introductory biology. *CBE–Life Sciences Education, 8*(3), 203–213. https://doi.org/10.1187/cbe.09-03-0025

Barron, B. J., Schwartz, D. J., Vye, N. J., Moore, A., Petrosino, A. J., Zech, L., Bransford, J. D., & the Cognition and Technology Group at Vanderbilt. (1998). Doing with understanding: Lessons from research on problem and project-based learning. *Journal of the Learning Sciences, 7*(3-4), 271–311. https://doi.org/10.1080/10508406.1998.9672056

Bell, P. (2019). Infrastructuring teacher learning about equitable science instruction. *Journal of Science Teacher Education, 30*(7), 681–690. https://doi.org/10.1080/1046560X.2019.1668218

Blikstein, P. (2018). Maker movement in education: History and prospects. In M. J. de Vries (Ed.), *Handbook of technology education* (pp. 419–437). Springer. https://doi.org/10.1007/978-3-319-44687-5

Boaler, J. (2002). *Experiencing school mathematics: Traditional and reform approaches to teaching and their impact on student learning.* Erlbaum.

Boaler, J. (2015). *What's math got to do with it? How parents and teachers can help children learn to love their least favorite subject* (2nd ed.). Penguin.

Boaler, J. (2016). *Mathematical mindsets: Unleashing students' potential through creative math, inspiring messages & innovative teaching.* Wiley.

Borrego, M., Nguyen, K., Crockett, C., DeMonbrun, R. M., Shekhar, P., Tharayil, S., Finelli, C. J., Rosenberg, R., & Waters, C. (2018, October 3–6). Systematic literature review of students' affective responses to active learning: Overview of results. In *IEEE Frontiers in Education Conference* (pp. 1–7). http://doi.org/10.1109/FIE.2018.8659306

Calabrese Barton, A., & Tan, E. (2018). A longitudinal study of equity-oriented STEM-rich making among youth from historically marginalized communities. *American Educational Research Journal, 55*(4), 761–800. https://doi.org/10.3102/0002831218758668

Cognition and Technology Group at Vanderbilt. (1992). The Jasper experiment: An exploration of issues in learning and instructional design. *Educational Technology Research and Development, 40*(1), 65–80. http://www.jstor.org/stable/30219998

Cognition and Technology Group at Vanderbilt. (1997). *The Jasper Project: Lessons in curriculum, instruction, assessment, and professional development.* Lawrence Erlbaum Associates Publishers

Cohen, G. L., & Sherman, D. K. (2014). The psychology of change: Self-affirmation and social psychological intervention. *Annual Review of Psychology, 65,* 333–371. https://doi.org/10.1146/annurev-psych-010213-115137

Committee on STEM Education of the National Science and Technology Council. (2018). *Charting a course for success: America's strategy for STEM education.* Executive Office of the President of the United States. https://www.energy.gov/sites/default/files/2019/05/f62/STEM-Education-Strategic-Plan-2018.pdf

Davis, E. A., & Krajcik, J. S. (2005). Designing educative curriculum materials to promote teacher learning. *Educational Researcher, 34*(3), 3–14. https://doi.org/10.3102/0013189X034003003

Edward, N. S. (2004). Evaluations of introducing project-based design activities in the first and second years of engineering courses. *European Journal of Engineering Education, 29*(4), 491–503. https://doi.org/10.1080/03043790410001716284

Ericson, B. (2018). *AP CS data for the United States 1998–2017: Detailed race and gender information 2017.* http://web.eecs.umich.edu/~mjguz/gacomputes/home.cc.gatech.edu/ice-gt/599

Esmonde, I., & Booker, A. N. (Eds.). (2016). *Power and privilege in the learning sciences: Critical and sociocultural theories of learning*. Routledge.

Fayer, S., Lacey, A., & Watson, A. (2017). *BLS spotlight on statistics: STEM occupations—Past, present, and future*. U.S. Department of Labor, Bureau of Labor Statistics.

Fields, D. A., & Kafai, Y. B. (2020). Hard fun with hands-on constructionist project-based learning. In S. Grover (Ed.), *Computer science in K–12: An A-to-Z handbook on teaching programming* (pp. 75–82). Edfinity.

Finelli, C. J., Nguyen, K., DeMonbrun, M., Borrego, M., Prince, M., Husman, J., Henderson, C., Shekhar, P., & Waters, C. K. (2018). Reducing student resistance to active learning: Strategies for instructors. *Journal of College Science Teaching*, 47(5), 80–91.

Finzer, B., & Wilkerson, M. (2020, Spring). Writing data stories. *Concord Newsletter*, 24(1), 10–11.

Frank, M., Lavy, I., & Elata, D. (2003). Implementing the project-based learning approach in an academic engineering course. *International Journal of Technology and Design Education*, 13(3), 273–288. https://doi.org/10.1023/A:1026192113732

Godhe, A.-L., Lilja, P., & Selwyn, N. (2019). Making sense of making: Critical issues in the integration of maker education into schools. *Technology, Pedagogy and Education*, 28(3), 317–328. https://doi.org/10.1080/1475939X.2019.1610040 https://doi.org/10.1080/1475939X.2019.1610040

Haase, W. (2016, September 28). Solving the project-based math conundrum: The multidimensional math classroom. *Education Week*. https://blogs.edweek.org/edweek/learning_deeply/2016/09/solving_the_project-based_math_conundrum_the_multidimensional_math_classroom.html

Hickey, D. T., Moore, A. L., & Pellegrino, J. W. (2001). The motivational and academic consequences of elementary mathematics environments: Do constructivist innovations and reforms make a difference? *American Educational Research Journal*, 38(3), 611–652. https://doi.org/10.3102/00028312038003611

Iscioglu, E., & Kale, I. (2010). An assessment of project based learning (PBL) environment based on the perceptions of students: A short course case study on circuit design for VLSI. *International Journal of Engineering Education*, 26(3), 564–572.

Krajcik, J. S., & Shin, N. (2022). Project-based learning. In R. K. Sawyer (Ed.), *The Cambridge handbook of learning sciences* (pp. 72–92). Cambridge University Press. https://doi.org/10.1017/9781108888295.006

Landivar, L. C. (2013). *The relationship between science and engineering education and employment in STEM occupations* (Report No. ACS-23). U.S. Census Bureau. https://www.census.gov/library/publications/2013/acs/acs-23.html

Lou, S.-J., Liu, Y.-H., Shih, R., Chuang, S.-Y., & Tseng, K. (2011). Effectiveness of on-line STEM project-based learning for female senior high school students. *International Journal of Engineering Education*, 27(2), 399–410.

Marshall, J. C., & Alston, D. M. (2014). Effective, sustained inquiry-based instruction promotes higher science proficiency among all groups: A five-year analysis. *Journal of Science Teacher Education*, 25(7), 807–821. https://doi.org/10.1007/s10972-014-9401-4

Martin, L. (2015). The promise of the maker movement for education. *Journal of Pre-College Engineering Education Research, 5*(1), 30–39. https://doi.org/10.7771/2157-9288.1099

Milesi, C., Perez-Felkner, L., Brown, K., & Schneider, B. (2017). Engagement, persistence, and gender in computer science: Results of a smartphone ESM study. *Frontiers in Psychology, 8,* Article 602. https://doi.org/10.3389/fpsyg.2017.00602

Miller, E. C., & Krajcik, J. S. (2019). Promoting deep learning through project-based learning: a design problem. *Disciplinary and Interdisciplinary Science Education Research, 1,* Article 7. https://doi.org/10.1186/s43031-019-0009-6

National Academies of Sciences, Engineering, and Medicine. (2018). *Learning through citizen science*: *Enhancing opportunities by design.* National Academies Press. https://doi.org/10.17226/25183 0

National Research Council. (2012). *A framework for K–12 science education: Practices, crosscutting concepts, and core ideas.* The National Academies Press.

Obama, B. (2013, May 9). *Remarks by the President at Manor New Technology High School* [Press release]. The White House. https://obamawhitehouse.archives.gov/the-press-office/2013/05/09/remarks-president-manor-new-technology-high-school

Palmer, S., & Hall, W. (2011). An evaluation of a project-based learning initiative in engineering education. *European Journal of Engineering Education, 36*(4), 357–365. https://doi.org/10.1080/03043797.2011.593095

Papert, S. (1980). *Mindstorms: Children, computers, and powerful ideas.* Basic Books.

Petrosino, A. J., Hughes, K., Sager, M. T., & Sherard., M. K. (2022). UTeach/NYC: A research practice partnership to expand and improve computer science education for all. *Proceedings of the 16th International Conference of the Learning Sciences—ICLS 2022.* Hiroshima, Japan: International Society of the Learning Sciences.

Petrosino, A. J., Sager, M. T., Washington, J., Sherard, M. K., Hughes, K., & Slabodsky, J. (2023, April). *Perceptions of CSforAll and project-based learning: Summary of findings from an RPP in NYC* [Roundtable session]. American Educational Research Association Annual Meeting, Chicago, Illinois, United States.

Prince, M. J., & Felder, R. M. (2006). Inductive teaching and learning methods: Definitions, comparisons, and research bases. *Journal of Engineering Education, 95*(2), 123–138. https://doi.org/10.1002/j.2168-9830.2006.tb00884.x

Savage, R. N., Chen, K. C., & Vanasupa, L. (2007). Integrating project-based learning throughout the undergraduate engineering curriculum. *Journal of STEM Education: Innovations and Research, 8*(3–4), 15–27.

Shekhar, P., & Borrego, M. (2017a). Examining instructional change: An observational study of engineering instructors' use of active learning. *International Journal of Engineering Education, 33*(6), 1717–1725.

Shekhar, P., & Borrego, M. (2017b). Implementing project-based learning in a civil engineering course: A practitioner's perspective. *International Journal of Engineering Education, 33*(4), 1138–1148.

Shekhar, P., Borrego, M., DeMonbrun, M., Finelli, C., Crockett, C., & Nguyen, K. (2020). Negative student response to active learning in STEM classrooms: A systematic review of underlying reasons. *Journal of College Science Teaching*, 49(6), 45–54. https://www.nsta.org/journal-college-science-teaching/journal-college-science-teaching-julyaugust-2020/negative-student

Steele, D. M., & Cohn-Vargas, B. (2013). *Identity safe classrooms: Places to belong and learn*. Corwin Press.

Tharayil, S., Borrego, M., Prince, M., Nguyen, K. A., Shekhar, P., Finelli, C. J., & Waters, C. (2018). Strategies to mitigate student resistance to active learning. *International Journal of STEM Education*, 5, Article 7. https://doi.org/10.1186/s40594-018-0102-y

University of Washington. (2019). *Leading the way to climate justice in education*. https://education.uw.edu/research-that-matters/2019/climate

Weintrop, D., Beheshti, E., Horn, M., Orton, K., Jona, K., Trouille, L., & Wilensky, U. (2016). Defining computational thinking for mathematics and science classrooms. *Journal of Science Education and Technology*, 25(1), 127–147. https://doi.org/10.1007/s10956-015-9581-5

Wilke, R. R. (2003). The effect of active learning on student characteristics in a human physiology course for nonmajors. *Advances in Physiology Education*, 27(1-4), 207–223. https://doi.org/10.1152/advan.00003.2002

Wlodkowski, R. J., & Ginsberg, M. B. (1995). *Diversity and motivation: Culturally responsive teaching*. Jossey-Bass.

Woodcock, C., Shekhar, P., & Huang-Saad, A. (2019). Examining project based entrepreneurship and engineering design course professional skills outcomes. *International Journal of Engineering Education*, 35(2), 631–644.

Woods, D., & Walkington, C. (2020). The evidence base behind the UTeach capstone course: Does project-based learning work? In J. Goodell & S. Koç (Eds.), *Preparing STEM teachers: The UTeach replication model* (pp. 241–258). Information Age Publishing.

Yadav, A., Subedi, D., Lunderberg, M., & Bunting, C. (2011). Problem-based learning: Influence on students' learning in an electrical engineering course. *Journal of Engineering Education*, 100(2), 253–280. https://doi.org/10.1002/j.2168-9830.2011.tb00013.x

Yeager, D. S., Hanselman, P., Walton, G. M., Murray, J., Crosnoe, R., Muller, C., Tipton, E., Schneider, B., Hulleman, C., Hinojosa, C. P., Paunesku, D., Romero, C., Flint, K., Robert, A., Trott, J., Iachan, R., Buontempo, J., Yang, S. M., Carvalho, C. M., ... Dweck, C. S. (2019). A national experiment reveals where a growth mindset improves achievement. *Nature*, 573, 364–369. https://doi.org/10.1038/s41586-019-1466-y

Zilberman, A., & Ice, L. (2021, January 19). Why computer occupations are behind strong STEM employment growth in the 2019–29 decade. *Beyond the Numbers: Employment & Unemployment*, 19(1). https://www.bls.gov/opub/btn/volume-10/why-computer-occupations-are-behind-strong-stem-employment-growth.htm

CHAPTER 6

PRACTICAL IMPLEMENTATION OF PBI AT SCALE

Administration and Assessment

In this chapter, we first discuss some of the dangers when implementing PBI at scale and the larger social and political context of PBI implementation. A challenge is the danger of popularity, including the pendulum swing of reform initiatives and an expansion of dubious or shallow implementations. Related to this, norms from modernist views of schooling can be incompatible with PBI, which better incorporates and builds upon postmodern views. We then discuss the critical importance we see in the education of district administrators for the successful implementation of PBI. Having the buy-in and investment of these leaders is critical to the success of any PBI initiative, as Gail Dickinson observed in the previous chapter. Demonstrating the impact of PBI on standardized assessments is also a large-scale implementation issue of particular importance. We discuss how a new approach to assessment known as pattern-based items offers some promise for PBI in high-stakes accountability situations.

DANGERS OF POPULARITY WHEN SCALING PBI

Putting the words "project based learning" or "project based instruction" into a search engine yields an incredible number of results. The vast majority of results will lead you to believe that PBI is a panacea of unlimited successful educational outcomes for all who embrace it. PBI can be exciting and transformative, but it is neither new nor are positive results assured. According to Strauss and Schneider (2018),

> In recent years, the approach has developed a significant following. One group, which calls itself High Quality Project Based Learning, boasts over 3,200 schools on its list of affiliates. PBL [project-based learning] has attracted millions of dollars in philanthropic funding from sources such as the Hewlett Foundation and the George Lucas Educational Foundation. A search for the phrase yields 15 million hits on the internet. (para. 6)

PBI saw its initial heyday over 100 years ago when William Kilpatrick heralded "the project method" as a way to help counter the then-popular aims of education as a way to ensure uniformity, efficiency, and emphasize memorization. Projects, as Kilpatrick envisioned and Dewey later embraced, directly challenged popular approach at the time, and these projects focused on depth, motivation, and engagement (Kliebard, 2004). Like now, teachers then were enthralled. When Kilpatrick spoke in Minneapolis, he sold out a local theater for three nights in a row. Strauss and Schneider (2018) stated,

> School administrators also began to promote projects—as a corrective to what the superintendent of the Cleveland schools called "the traditional fact-cramming method." In declaring his support for the project method, Milwaukee's superintendent contrasted it with "Fordizing" children—a reference to the assembly-line manufacture of automobiles.
>
> Displeased with an emphasis on "fact-cramming," educators of the 1920s embraced the project method. The heyday of the project method, in turn, led directly to concerns about curricular rigor. That next period, which produced the classic breadth-oriented curriculum, the Advanced Placement program, ended with a pendulum swing back toward projects and authentic tasks. Eventually it swung away again.
>
> The present infatuation with PBI, or any of its close cousins—expeditionary learning, problem-based learning, deeper learning, and so on—is the predictable response to the standards and accountability movement that has dominated public education for the past two decades. (para. 13–15)

The return of the project method, then, is merely evidence that the policy pendulum has begun its downswing. If projects are to withstand the test of time, advocates would be wise to remember why reforms appear cyclically. Strauss and Schneider (2018) stated, "The further the pendulum swings in one direction, the faster it will swing in the other. Perhaps, this time, a little equilibrium is in order" (para. 25).

One group focused on PBI attested to the popularity of the approach: the group trained 500 educators in project-based learning in 2010; in 2016, the group trained 15,000, and by 2020 the number reported on its website was 190,000. This same nonprofit has established partnerships with 60 school districts over the same time span (Zubrzycki, 2016).

We note that the course Project-Based Instruction in the UTeach Natural Sciences program was initiated in 1999. Currently, 42 colleges and universities offer the UTeach course Project-Based Instruction. Over 7,900 pre- and in-service teachers have taken the course. Eighty sections of this course have been offered at the University of Texas at Austin, and over 500 sections of the course have been offered at the 42 UTeach replication sites around the country. We now estimate that almost 800,000 high school students are taught by UTeach-educated teachers nationally, all teachers with experience in the theory and the pedagogy of PBI. UTeach was addressing PBI well before the current resurgence in popularity and promotion.

Of concern are increases in offerings of instructional materials that claim to be project based but do not fit the standards of "Big P" (some also call this a "gold standard" or the "strong" PBI standard). Teachers face difficulties in finding the time to learn about PBI and to create meaningful projects while trying to address accountability standards and work within the existing school day schedule and calendar. Further, some schools use PBI only with students who are either high or low performing. We can see the many challenges of the popularity of PBI. We must be cautious of shallow implementations of PBI that seek to promote the sizzle but not the substance. This need for implementation with fidelity will continue to be a growing concern. In the words of Dr. John Bransford, Professor Emeritus of Learning Sciences and Psychology at the University of Washington and member of the National Academy of Education, "I'd rather a student receive a good lecture than a bad project." Our commitment must be to assure students have access to challenging, engaging, and intellectually rigorous PBI.

CHALLENGES TO PBI FROM SYSTEMS STEEPED IN THE MODERNIST TRADITION

One of the primary barriers to implementing PBI at scale is the deep philosophical differences between the norms of "traditional" schooling and the reimagined norms that must be in place for PBI to be successful. One useful way to think of the contrast between these two approaches is to compare modernist and postmodernist perspectives. As PBI centers on the relationship of STEM to peoples' lived experiences, it requires a fundamental shift in curricular thinking. Curriculum developers may need to turn from the intellectual study of a discipline for its own sake to the study of its relationships to human life and action (DeBoer, 1991).

To discuss this shift, we go back to early curriculum development. Perhaps no single person has had as much impact on how the American curriculum is thought about, structured, and communicated than Ralph W. Tyler. Tyler (1949) formalized his thoughts on viewing, analyzing, and interpreting the curriculum and instructional program in *Basic Principles of Curriculum and Instruction*. This book remains a bestseller and has been reprinted in 36 editions, shaping curriculum and instructional design to this day. The book presents a deceptively simple structure for delivering and evaluating instruction, consisting of four parts that have become known as the Tyler rationale. Tyler embodies the approach of modernism[1] to the field of curriculum. Tyler presents four basic questions to the field:

1. What educational purposes should the school seek to attain? (Objectives)
2. What educational experiences can be provided that are likely to attain these purposes? (Design)
3. How can these educational experiences be effectively organized? (Scope and sequence)
4. How can we determine whether these purposes are being attained? (Evaluation)

Tyler, with his embrace of modernism, spoke a simple language. That simplicity was manifested primarily in a conceptualization of curriculum planning that could be reduced to a series of steps. This, in essence, was the scientific backing that modernism needed to counter more complex efforts of education envisioned by Kilpatrick and John Dewey with their "projects." Tyler introduced a modernistic language and methodology to curriculum development that facilitated the introduction of curriculum making into the second half of the 20th century and well into the current century. The Tyler rationale gave a clear vision. This orientation allowed developers to believe they were following the right path. Problems could be identified, determination of objectives could be made, necessary experiences could be selected, and assurances could be made that what was initiated was now completed (Cornbleth, 1990).

With the Tyler four-step process, the field had firmly established itself with a rubric for curriculum development that appeared to be both scientific and technological. But now a new theme is beginning to emerge in the discussions of science educators as well as curriculum developers. Scientific literacy and the integration of science with the rest of human life and with other academic disciplines were phases indicating a shift away from the intellectual study of the structure of a discipline for its own sake and a renewed emphasis on the study of science in its relationships to human life and action (DeBoer, 1991). A new perspective introduced by Doll (1993) and influenced greatly by Iiya Prigogine's chaos theory (Prigogine & Stengers, 1984) is challenging the modernistic, scientific-rationale view of natural phenomena as well as curriculum making in general. According to

Pinar et al. (1995), the 50 years of curriculum development since 1945 were reconceptualized from modernism and Tyler to postmodernism and Doll.

The argument for going beyond modernism is not to criticize the work of Tyler or other curriculum theorists but simply to recognize that we live in different times. The modernists reflected a particular view of the world in which life could be analogically conceptualized as mechanical, where a stable and predictable universe existed, the process of curriculum development (or any other human activity) could be compartmentalized and decontextualized, and goals could be separated from the experiences designed to address those goals (Hunkins & Hammill, 1994). In this view, modernism could be thought of as a mechanical clock.

Current thinking is that life is organic, not mechanical; the universe is dynamic, not stable; the process of curriculum development is not a passive acceptance of steps, but evolves from the interaction of components within the system in specific contexts; and goals emerge often from the very experiences in which people engage. In the words of Cornbleth (1990), "Curriculum gains life as it is enacted." To look beyond the modernists and the Tyler approach, we must think about curriculum development from a holistic approach and consider the dynamics of the entire system. In such cases, as Lewin (1992) suggested, order will emerge from the dynamic. The system contains internal dynamics that make it both complex and adaptive, creating opportunities. Using the metaphors of biology (environment, organic) over the language of mechanics (clocks, machines) recognizes that diversity and differentiation are commonplace (Toulmin, 1990). The biology metaphor enables the consideration of the curriculum and its creation as comprising a living system. Rather than thinking about the manipulation of separate and distinct parts, we accept that we are creating new environments. As Waldrop (1993) explained from the postmodern perspective, we recognize and celebrate curricula as organic—a living system that never really settles down and becomes static. Curricula are seen as having a certain amount of perpetual novelty. In the same manner, Krajcik et al. (1998) discussed the need for multiple iterations of a project-based curriculum, and Polman (2000) wrote of the need for a continually evolving curriculum. The curricula, as well as the learning environment as a whole, contain internal dynamics that make them both complex and adaptive, allowing for numerous possibilities.

Firmly rooted in postmodernism thought, Doll (1993) suggested an alternative to the modernist rationale for curriculum development and, most importantly, a perspective for curriculum development within PBI. Doll presented four criteria for a curriculum designed to advance a postmodern view: richness, recursion, relations, and rigor. In dealing with richness, developers (teachers, students, and interested parties from the wider community) must reflect upon the depth of the curriculum that can be experienced to enrich students' lives. The right amount cannot be determined but rather must be continually negotiated between the teachers, the students, and the text. Yet, Doll asserted, one aspect cannot be negotiated: The curriculum must have some distinctive qualities (benchmark, dilemma lesson, etc.).

The second criterion for a postmodern curriculum is recursion. A recursive process in curriculum development enables the participants to engage in reflective interaction with the entire learning community. The very act of curriculum development not only enables a listing of curricular possibilities for students to experience, but also creates a shared culture for all participants. In creating a curriculum, there is no fixed beginning or end. The curriculum is designed to allow for continually going back to and then utilizing previous points and insights into a growing sense of understanding.

The third criterion, relations, suggests that in designing a postmodern curriculum, the relations between the parts of the curriculum need to be addressed, rather than focusing on the individual parts of the system. This emphasis on relations brings students and teachers into dialogue. The criterion of relations makes obvious that curriculum making is a social activity played out in particular frameworks; it is a human activity full of surprises (Cornbleth, 1990). This approach differs significantly from the technically inspired approach of listing steps with the false comfort of assuring no surprises. With these relations, participants join the dialogue based on their contexts and experiences, The process of creating curricula is then seen as interactive. People can participate in a type of ecological system, able to be both adaptive and self-regulatory (Hunkins & Hammill, 1994).

The fourth criterion is rigor. Rigor is not a step in the process and is better thought of as a criterion to consider when developing a curriculum. Rigor demands that developers be aware (a) of the assumptions they bring to the curriculum design process; (b) that assumptions contain values that influence the curriculum process as well as the learning environment; and (c) that there is no "right" answer to curriculum development but rather a search for new combinations, interpretations, and patterns (Doll, 1993).

Curriculum development from a postmodern perspective is ecological in view (see, for instance, Greeno, 1991, for negotiating in a mathematical "environment"). It is self-organizing as opposed to mechanistic, is nonlinear as opposed to linear, and draws its essence from chaos theory rather than Newtonian mechanics. However, the new paradigm is not the antithesis of the modern perspective. The new model is more of an acceptance of complexities and hybridization of the modern. Rather than denying our modernist past, we are adding to its complexity and creativity. The approach and perspective to curriculum development should be more of a transformational process than a revolution.

Compared to Kilpatrick's (1918) notion of the project method or Dewey's (1902) conceptually complex version of occupations, modernism spoke a simple language. That simplicity was manifested primarily in a conceptualization of curriculum planning that could be reduced to a series of steps. This, in essence, was the scientific backing that modernism needed to counter the efforts of Dewey. Social efficiency held out the promise of social stability during a time when institutions such as the family and the church were seen as being in decline. The content of the curriculum had to be changed to draw a tight connection between what was taught in school and the adult activities students would one day be called upon to perform. The curriculum would become a science of exact measurement and precise standards, which would then maintain societal order (Kliebard, 2004).

Unable to explain complex physical or psychological phenomena through a simple reductionist paradigm, chaos theory, complex adaptive systems, and systems theory emerged. In its wake, a postmodern paradigm began to develop. Influences of such a position are only beginning to be addressed in the field of education (Pinar et al., 1995). While not abandoning the advances of the past, postmodernism presents a way to look at a classroom as an organic, complex, adaptive system.

Paradigms do not change overnight. Some take years, decades, and even centuries. But a paradigm shift is taking place in our awareness of the interconnections of our world. PBI embraces this complexity but is handcuffed by a relic from modernism—the standard Tyler-inspired "lesson plan" or curriculum guide, which is linear and reductionistic and offers a false sense of "order." Any realistic and vibrant enactment of PBI going forward will need to reconcile the current tension between modernism and postmodernism in terms of curriculum development and enactment as well as pedagogical instructional strategies. This is an approach more consistent with work influenced in the learning sciences by both design experiments (Brown, 1992; Glaser, 1994) and the idea of learning environments (Collins et al., 1994).

Too often when we hear "postmodern" we somehow think of something that is "other" to our experience. When this idea was proposed by one of the authors at a conference, a collective sigh permeated the room. Many have a knee-jerk reaction to the term *postmodern*.[1] Yet, the more we read about it and thought of our own experiences, the more it seemed to offer some explanatory coherence to the process of curricula development in project-based classrooms. Thus, rigor is a vital aspect of PBI and requires that developers be aware of (a) their assumptions; (b) their values that influence the curriculum process as well as the learning environment; and (c) that curriculum development involves no single right answer but rather a search for new combinations, interpretations, and patterns. This rigor then requires deep domain knowledge as well as sequential understanding of the enacted curriculum.

Ultimately, the main argument is PBI, as it evolves in cognitive research, affords some exciting possibilities for the future. PBI centers on the relationship of STEM to peoples' lives and experiences, requiring curriculum developers, educators, principals, and superintendents to shift how they think about the curriculum.

SUPERINTENDENTS AND PBI AT SCALE

What Superintendents Need to Know About How People Learn

We three authors have spent the better part of our professional lives working in numerous ways on PBI. We have developed curricula and assessment items and have researched various components of PBI such as experimentation, data modeling, technology, and teacher education. The focus of much of this work has been either the student or the teacher, like much of the field in writings about PBI. However, when the first author served as an assistant superintendent of schools, he observed a large and noticeable research gap in the area of PBI. Specifically, there needs to be a focus on district leadership for PBI to have any chance of long-term success. This means a focus on the education of superintendents, board members, and district leaders such as directors and supervisors.

As part of this commitment, beginning during the summer of 2015, the first author began teaching a course to aspiring district leaders as part of the University of Texas at Austin's Cooperative Superintendency Program. The Cooperative Superintendency Program is at the forefront of preparing education leaders to meet the ever-changing needs of the public education system. The dedicated faculty and intensive coursework maintain the program's position among the top-rated superintendency preparation programs in the nation. The program seeks to attract leaders with outstanding professional readiness and prepare them for executive-level positions, including superintendents of school districts, chief executives in state education agencies, directors in education service centers or laboratories, and executive-level management posts in large cities or suburban districts.

The unofficial title of the course is What Superintendents Need to Know About How People Learn. This course focuses on what education leaders (particularly district leadership) should know about "how people learn" and the implementation of advanced pedagogies, such as PBI, at scale in the accountability era of the No Child Left Behind Act and beyond. The course concentrates on both theory and case studies of districts, with a fair number of outside experts with experience in PBI integrated into the class.

In the past, the class was visited by former superintendents of schools and a nationally recognized school leader in PBI implementation and engaged in activities involving personal digital devices and agent-based modeling with advanced technologies. The course synthesizes the scientific basis of STEM learning. The scientific achievements include a fuller understanding of (a) memory and the structure of knowledge; (b) problem-solving and reasoning; (c) the early foundations of learning; (d) regulatory processes that govern learning, including metacognition; and (e) how symbolic thinking emerges from the culture and community of the learner. Until superintendents truly understand how people learn and how thoughtfully implemented PBI embraces how people learn, widespread and systemic successful implementation of PBI is unlikely. This is true especially when superintendents impose pressure to "raise test scores," or directors and boards of education do not fully appreciate what it means to experience inquiry. In the class, aspiring superintendents shoot off model rockets, create and monitor two-tier terrariums, estimate the mass of a tree and the amount of CO_2 absorbed, and utilize agent-based programming to model phenomena.

Whether the goal is for PBI to happen from time to time or daily, in one school building or across an entire school system, getting positive results demands informed leadership. To be clear, our approach is in contrast to many domain-independent and generalized notions of administrative support for PBI, which often include such "little p" or theory-light suggestions as "be strategic," "lay a foundation," "build teacher ownership," "share success," and "stay patient" (Larmer et al., 2015).

How to Introduce PBI to Future and Current Superintendents

All of the aspiring superintendents were in class to discuss the potential for PBI implementation at the district level. Future superintendents watched an informational video describing the history and development of PBI and agent-based modeling technologies. Afterward, they had the opportunity to work with computer simulations. The future superintendents spent the class discussing the implications, challenges, and benefits of district-wide implementation of a group- and computer-based Project.

The opportunity to demo the PBI technologies with future district leaders is exciting for two reasons. First, it exponentially increases the radius of implementation; each future superintendent who is interested in using PBI capabilities in their district has the potential of reaching thousands of students. Second, we can place our approach and technology in the hands of actual users, to discover more about its limitations and capabilities.

Session 1: Introducing Computer Models to PBI. We presented PBI capabilities as a way to unlock the true potential by providing an easy-to-use, easy-to-author platform for exploring and learning about emergent phenomena. Emergence is a way of thinking about many systemic phenomena, for example, how birds flock or how ecosystems change over time. However, exploring emergent phenomena in the classroom may be hindered by time or resource constraints. We demonstrated agent-based PBI models developed to explore the extinction of wolves and its impact on elk and aspen populations. We describe this approach further in our final chapter.

Session 2: Framework for Integrated PBI in STEM Disciplines. We began a presentation highlighting the ability of PBI simulations to unlock curricula commonly inaccessible through more traditional forms of representation. We began by discussing an issue we encountered while teaching using PBI in the previous year: Student-generated driving questions were shallow in terms of rigor and followed a nominally generative frame for engagement. We went on to discuss how emergent phenomena like the extinction of a species are complex and require the ability to model multiple agents and their individual behaviors, which is beyond the scope of typical ecological models like the diorama or food web typically used in K–12 instruction. We demonstrated multiple models made and edited by preservice teachers to explore the complex variables involved in an apex predator's extinction. Once participants had a chance to explore the models, they were encouraged to discuss other driving questions that could be related to this content. The budding superintendents came up with these driving questions:

- What happens to the genetic diversity of the wolf population upon reintroduction?
- How do wolf and elk reproduction rates differ, and how does this impact the population?
- How similar or dissimilar were the reintroduction efforts of the panther in South Florida?
- How does the building of a road or other human-made barrier change the dynamics of this model?
- What about farmers? What are the impacts of humans who hunt and protect their cattle in the Yellowstone ecosystem?
- Which amount of wolves produces a steady-state equilibrium? What about a dynamic equilibrium?

Quickly, participants realized the fractal nature of using simulations and models. Users can continually ask more refined questions and author new simulations to explore these questions—a central feature of PBI. Towards the end of the class, we demonstrated the potential of integrating PBI with GeoGebra, one of the most widely used online mathematics platform for algebra and geometry. The aspiring superintendents were excited by the model's ability to bring exploration into the variables that produce similar-area triangles and wanted to see more mathematics examples.

Subsequent discussions about the activity indicated a more detailed and personal sense of what PBI actually is and the kind of support and time needed to allow such deep disciplinary knowledge to develop. The aspiring superintendents uniformly spoke of having a much better understanding, appreciation, and sense of the potential for PBI in a district. This case can provide guidance for others interested in supporting administrators in understanding PBI and its strengths.

ASSESSMENT

Perhaps the most important consideration for PBI at scale is assessment. Results of assessments are a primary way in which implementations receive continued buy-in and support (Harris et al., 2016; Pellegrino et al., 2016). However, traditional standardized tests may be insensitive to instruction (Popham et al., 2014) or not be ideal for improving future instruction based on past achievement data. For assessment-based accountability to improve educational outcomes for all students, assessment results must identify effective instruction (National Research Council, 2001). Only then can these results be used to improve instruction. Rather than allowing for a deficit mindset to reinforce inequities in education, which have long-term implications for the lives of underserved students, assessment-based accountability was intended to be a key driver of reform in the original No Child Left Behind legislation and its successors.

Pattern-based items are being developed to provide a significant, and fully scalable, alternative to current dichotomously scored and analyzed items. For an individual assessment question with four responses (A, B, C, or D), both multiselect and pattern-based items allow the students to select, or endorse, more than one response (e.g., A and C or B, C, and D). With a standard multiselect item, however, only one combination, the "exact match," is scored as correct (1). All other combinations are scored as incorrect (0). Although legacy multiselect multiple-choice items can be viewed as an improvement over the more commonly used single-select multiple-choice items, the dichotomous scoring, and subsequent analyses, for both single-select and multiselect items continues to be based on only two states: either 1 or 0, right or wrong.

In contrast, pattern-based items were developed to work with the full combinatoric space of student responses. For pattern-based items with four responses, there are 16 possible selection combinations (15 if "no response" is not included). Rather than continue the current practice of reducing these states to only the two states of right or wrong, pattern-based items provide significant, actionable insights related to student learning outcomes (16 states vs. two states). Some of the advantages of pattern-based items are the following:

1. Pattern-based items yield more information. The patterns generated (and information provided) by one pattern-based item are equal to eight items created by other testing models.
2. More standards can be covered. Because pattern-based items generate more information, such items can cover more standards in fewer questions.
3. Shorter assessments mean more teaching time. With fewer items on each test, the average pattern-based item test takes around 30 minutes to complete. In comparison, traditional tests take up to 8 hours to complete.
4. Pattern-based items offer rapid results and built-in feedback. Pattern-based items and the related technology being developed can provide clear feedback to teachers and students about their results immediately after the tests are completed. Instant results and built-in feedback are superior to months-long processing and little feedback, with teachers often getting results for tests only after their students have moved on to the next grade level.

As mentioned previously, with a traditional test item, the answer is either right or wrong—either full credit or no credit. That kind of item only provides two possible pieces of information about the student's understanding. In contrast, a pattern-based item has 16 possible answer combinations and offers the teacher eight times as much information about the student's knowledge as the traditional item. The difference is not just the quantity of information. In a pattern-based item, the choices show different patterns of student understanding. For example, one of the correct choices may demonstrate basic grade-level comprehension, and another correct choice may call for more advanced grasp of a concept. One correct choice may demonstrate knowledge of one thinking skill, whereas another correct answer relies on another thinking skill.

Consequently, each answer combination provides the teacher with a detailed view of the student's strengths and weaknesses in understanding the content. For example, in mathematics, an item may ask the student to choose among four different ways of expressing the fraction 3/4. The correct answers might be (a) 1/4 + 1/4 + 1/4 and (b) .75. If the student answers only (a) 1/4 + 1/4 + 1/4, the teacher knows that the student understands how to add fractions but likely not how to convert fractions into decimals. The teacher can use that information to help the student learn. During the next class session, the teacher can reinforce the student for adding fractions correctly and then guide the student to review converting fractions into decimals. If the student gives both correct answers, the teacher knows the student understands both concepts. Pattern-based items often include teacher notes and student feedback for every choice on every item, making comprehension and usability issues clear for teachers. The teacher can use this information almost instantly, because software collects and analyses the class's responses as soon as the test ends. In this way, the same students who took the test can learn by examining their answers. Compare this to the usual standardized assessment, where the student does not get the chance to work with their own test results and thus learns little from these assessment events.

Pattern-based items have other advantages. Because so much more information results per item, these types of tests can be significantly shorter than old-fashioned standardized tests. Standardized tests are not very exciting; less time on tests means more time engaging in learning. See Figure 6.1 for an example of a pattern-based test item in engineering.

Figure 6.1

Example of a Pattern-Based Item

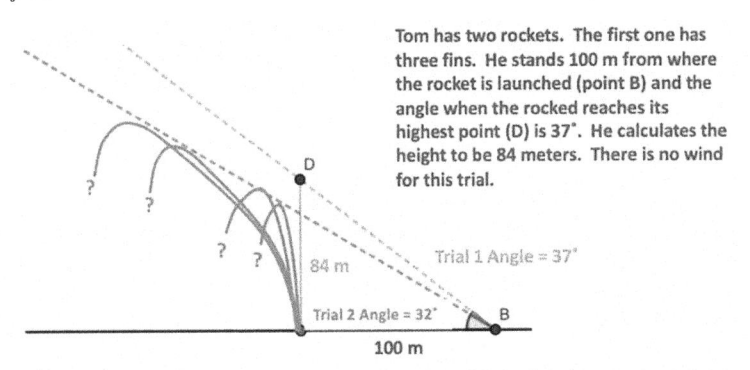

Tom has two rockets. The first one has three fins. He stands 100 m from where the rocket is launched (point B) and the angle when the rocked reaches its highest point (D) is 37°. He calculates the height to be 84 meters. There is no wind for this trial.

Trial 1 Angle = 37°
Trial 2 Angle = 32°
84 m
100 m

Later, when he fires his second rocket with four fins, it is windy and the rocket does not go straight up like it did for his first rocket. Tom measures the angle at the highest point to be 32°.

What could he do next

[A] Conclude that the second rocket with four fins did not go as high as the first rocket with three fins
[B] Fire the first rocket again while the wind is still blowing
[C] Fire the second rocket again when the wind stops blowing
[D] Estimate the distance B is from where the second rocket reached its highest point and then calculate the height

In conclusion, a model of PBI that scales across districts has been elusive, despite widespread enthusiasm for the approach. Strong district leadership, a coherent and research-informed vision of PBI, an appropriate underlying model of the role of curriculum, and new approaches to assessment will be needed for PBI to reach its promise at scale. Changes need to happen at every level of the system, including how curricula are organized and conceptualized, how assessments are designed, and how school leaders understand and provide support for new instructional approaches.

REFERENCES

Brown, A. L. (1992). Design experiments: Theoretical and methodological challenges in creating complex interventions in classroom settings. *Journal of the Learning Sciences, 2*(2), 141–178. https://doi.org/10.1207/s15327809jls0202_2

Collins, A., Greeno, J. G., & Resnick, L. B. (1994). Learning environments. In T. Husen & T. N. Postlewaite (Eds.), *International encyclopedia of education* (2nd ed., pp. 3297–3302). Pergamon.

Cornbleth, C. (1990). *Curriculum in context.* Falmer Press.

DeBoer, G. E. (1991). *A history of ideas in science education: Implications for practice.* Teachers College Press.

Dewey, J. (1902). *The child and the curriculum.* University of Chicago Press.

Doll, W., Jr. (1993). *A post-modern perspective on curriculum.* Teachers College Press.

Glaser, R. (1994). Instructional technology and the measurement of learning outcomes: Some questions. *Educational Measurement: Issues and Practice, 13*, 6–8. https://doi.org/10.1111/j.1745-3992.1994.tb00561.x

Greeno, J. G. (1991). Number sense as situated knowing in a conceptual domain. *Journal for Research in Mathematics Education, 22*(3), 170–218. https://doi.org/10.2307/749074

Harris, C. J., Krajcik, J. S., Pellegrino, J. W., & McElhaney, K. W. (2016). *Constructing assessment tasks that blend disciplinary core ideas, crosscutting concepts, and science practices for classroom formative applications.* SRI International.

Hunkins, F., & Hammill, P. (1994). Beyond Tyler and Taba: Reconceptualizing the curriculum process. *Peabody Journal of Education, 69*(3), 4–18. https://doi.org/10.1080/01619569409538774

Kilpatrick, W. H. (1918). The project method. *Teachers College Record, 19*(4), 319–335.

Kliebard, H. M. (2004). *The struggle for the American curriculum: 1893–1958* (3rd ed.). RoutledgeFalmer.

Krajcik, J., Blumenfeld, P., Marx R. W., Bass, K. M., Fredericks, J., & Soloway, E. (1998). Inquiry in project-based science classrooms: Initial attempts by middle school students. *Journal of the Learning Sciences, 7*(3–4), 313–350. https://doi.org/10.1080/10508406.1998.9672057

Larmer, J., Mergendoller, J. R., & Boss, S. (2015). *Setting the standard for project based learning: A proven approach to rigorous classroom instruction.* ASCD.

Lewin, R. (1992). *Complexity: Life at the edge of chaos.* Macmillan.

National Research Council. (2001). *Knowing what students know: The science and design of educational assessment.* National Academies Press.

Pellegrino, J. W., DiBello, L. V., & Goldman, S. R. (2016). A framework for defining and evaluating the validity of instructionally relevant assessments. *Educational Psychologist, 51*(1), 59–81. https://doi.org/10.1080/00461520.2016.1145550

Pinar, W. F., Reynolds, W. M., Slattery, P., & Taubman, P. M. (1995). *Understanding curriculum: An introduction to the study of historical and contemporary curriculum discourses.* Peter Lang.

Polman, J. L. (2000). *Designing project-based science: Connecting learners through guided inquiry.* Teachers College Press.

Popham, W. J., Berliner, D. C., Neal, M., Kingston, S. H., Fuhrman, S. M., Jeffrey, L., & Chatterji, C. M. (2014). Can today's standardized achievement tests yield instructionally useful data? *Quality Assurance in Education, 22*(4), 303–318. https://doi.org/10.1108/QAE-07-2014-0033

Selznick, P. (1992). *The moral commonwealth: Social theory and the promise of community.* University of California Press.

Strauss, V., & Schneider, J. (2018, December 12). Project-based learning is a new rage in education. Never mind that it's a century old. *Washington Post.* https://www.washingtonpost.com/education/2018/12/12/project-based-learning-is-new-rage-education-never-mind-that-its-century-old/

Toulmin, S. (1990). *Cosmopolis: The hidden agenda of modernity.* University of Chicago Press.

Tyler, R. W. (1949). *Basic principles of curriculum and instruction.* University of Chicago Press.

Waldrop, M. M. (1993). *Complexity: The emerging science at the edge of order and chaos.* Simon & Schuster.

Zubrzycki, J. (2016, July 22). As project-based learning gains in popularity, experts offer caution. *Education Week.* https://blogs.edweek.org/edweek/curriculum/2016/07/as_project-based_learning_gain.html

ENDNOTE

1. Modernism is often erroneously attributed to contemporary society (Selznick, 1992). If this were so, all societies or social institutions would be modern in their time. In fact, modernism dates to the time of Sir Isaac Newton. The predominant characteristics of this movement is the emphasis on the rational, the objective, and the separation of thought and action. It is a society that chooses to utilize the rational and scientific in addressing the problems facing human life and the society (Toulmin, 1990). Having achieved its height during the 20th century, it is no surprise that modernism would find a place in education, specifically in curriculum (Doll, 1993).

CHAPTER 7

THE FUTURE OF PBI CURRICULA

Issues of Technology and Community

We conclude this book by looking forward to some of the most important, exciting, and pressing issues for the future of PBI, focusing particularly on curricular issues. First, we discuss opportunities related to emerging technologies and their use in activities, such as virtual reality (VR) field trips and agent-based modeling. Then, we close the chapter by considering the potential of PBI to promote equity and access through the centering of community resources.

EMERGING TECHNOLOGIES FOR PBI

As we finish this final chapter, instruction in K–12 schools and higher education has shifted to more virtual instruction, which has large implications for the implementation of PBI in STEM. Field experiences where students can investigate STEM concepts in real-world settings—like parks, museums, gardens, urban centers, and different ecological areas—are a central component of many approaches to PBI. Virtual field experiences, where students explore these environments through media like photos and videos, have become increasingly prevalent, although the degree to which these online resources are available for different sites and communities can vary. Managing student collaboration around complex tasks has become more challenging but also more sought after, with interactive shared documents accessible by students and teachers, small-group video meetings taking on new levels of significance, and the logistics of project management becoming more complex. Shifting to digital rather than physical tools represents a new learning curve for both students and teachers. For example, teachers are shifting from using a compass and ruler in geometry projects to fully using virtual simulation environments like Desmos or GeoGebra. Virtual experiments and simulations of physical, biological, or chemical phenomena can offer some substitute for laboratory experiences if designed well but may not be widely available for all topics. Virtual reality technology may emerge as a powerful way to immerse students and teachers virtually in STEM explorations and environments (e.g., Walkington et al., 2021). Walkington et al. (2021) demonstrated how a collaborative virtual reality experience centered on geometric modeling can change the way mathematics teachers think about how technology can support collaboration, critical thinking around dynamic geometry relationships, and the role and relevance of technology to math learning.

Self-paced learning of STEM skills where students work progressively through virtual tasks until they reach mastery (like in intelligent tutoring systems) likely will increase in practice in schools. These tools can be effectively leveraged in PBI approaches, if they allow students to seek out and learn new knowledge in a "just-in-time" fashion as the need arises as they are progressing through Project work. However, when used as part of PBI approaches, this kind of individual skill development and practice should be embedded in larger, richer tasks and should be learned for authentic Project needs. In the remainder of this section, we discuss two important trends in technology and PBI: virtual field trips and cloud-based computing.

Implementing Field Trips in PBI

Using field trips to collect scientific data outside of the classroom to help address a driving question is a common feature of our teacher education course on PBI. Field trips can function as a way to "launch" a PBI unit by immersing students in a real-world problem or need in an organization or site (e.g., launching a math PBI unit on tiny houses by having students visit a tiny home exhibit). Whether it is a trip to a museum, a nearby stream, or the high school stadium to shoot off model rockets, opportunities to collect data and conduct experiments outside of the traditional classroom are an integral aspect of PBI. However, teachers are generally not taught how to orchestrate and implement field trips as part of their pedagogical training (Behrendt & Franklin, 2014). As a result, inexperienced teachers may be unaware that students benefit from contextual learning that takes place before, during, and after the field trip (Falk & Dierking, 2016).

This pedagogical sequence is important because it allows the teacher to scaffold a field trip that is rooted in students' prior experiences, interest, and knowledge. Without appropriate planning, students can be overwhelmed by the novelty of the new experience, leading to heavy cognitive load and a reduction in desired learning outcomes (Falk et al., 1978). During the field trip, student learning can be enhanced through the guidance of a docent (i.e., a museum volunteer, employee, or teacher who acts as a guide) and through interactions with displays, exhibits, and kiosks (Metz, 2005). After the visit, the teacher can help reinforce the experience and enhance recall by engaging students in discussion, activities, readings, and videos (Behrendt & Franklin, 2014).

Implementing field trips as part of a preservice elementary science method course provides an opportunity to engage in contextual learning while also modeling the pedagogical sequence. Preservice elementary teachers often lack confidence in their science teaching abilities (Howitt, 2007), but elementary science method courses have been shown to develop preservice teachers' beliefs, attitudes, and self-efficacy towards science (Kazempour & Sadler, 2015). These courses introduce preservice teachers to science pedagogy while also exposing them to activities beyond the walls of the classroom, including workshops, family days, and field trips (Kisiel, 2013). During these trips, students can develop their conceptual understanding of scientific concepts, while also assessing the advantages and disadvantages of museum-based field trips (Morentin & Guisasola, 2015).

Even with this pedagogical training, however, the advantages of these visits may never be realized if the teacher goes on to teach in a school where time, budget, and testing constraints make field trips impossible. The possibility of virtual field trips adds a new dimension to teacher preparation to implement field trips. Thus, we turn our attention to virtual field trips, their affordances and constraints, and how other researchers have studied them. The findings described in this section are specifically related to the sequencing of pre- versus post- virtual field trips with in-person museum field trips, the use of local experiences, recommendations to reduce virtual reality fatigue, and emerging equity issues related to virtual field trips.

Sequencing of In-Person and Virtual Field Trips

In a virtual reality field trip, students can explore a fully virtually rendered, immersive digital space using a headset or other device that can project a virtual world onto students' surroundings or immersive students in experiencing or traveling through a 3D rendered virtual environment. Based on the findings of a study conducted by Harron et al. (2019), virtual-reality field trips are best used for recall of the field trip experience after an in-person field trip. This study compared students who experienced the VR field trip before the in-person field trip to those who experienced it after. The before museum field trip group exhibited less exploration in the VR environment, possibly due to being unfamiliar with the environment—a finding that aligns with the novelty effect identified by Falk et al. (1978). Participants in the postmuseum virtual field trip group showed higher levels of recall from their in-person field trip, particularly when seeking out their favorite exhibits. In addition, participants in the post-museum group more freely explored the virtual space and sought to explore parts of the museum they had not seen on the in-person trip, such as the fourth floor. As such, the ways local and virtual field trip experiences can be used to complement each other may need to be considered.

Opportunity to Rethink the Local Field Trip Experience

Although participants in this study visited a local museum, virtual reality was still perceived as a way to visit "far away" places, rather than as a supplementary tool to enhance local field trips. Further work needs to be done so the posttrip benefits of virtual reality can be fully utilized in the classroom with more museums, zoos, and other popular field trip destinations. Numerous user-friendly advances have occurred since the custom software for this study (Harron et al., 2019) was developed. First, many locations have already been captured as 360-degree photospheres and can be viewed in virtual reality using the Google Street View app on both Android and iOS devices. Virtual reality in Street View was not an option when the study was conducted but has since opened the door to Google's vast image collection to be used in virtual field trips. A second solution could include students using 360-degree cameras to capture their own 360-degree photos or video while they are on the field trip. The photos or video can be viewed after the field trip using the application included with the camera. This strategy would provide an opportunity to give students authorship over their virtual experience.

Scaffolding to Reduce Virtual-Reality Fatigue

After only about 10 minutes of using low-cost virtual-reality technologies, virtual reality fatigue begins to set in for students (Harron et al., 2019). As such, educators should consider how they plan to implement the virtual experience in the classroom. Given that 10 minutes is not long enough to explore larger destinations, such as a four-story museum of natural history, teachers may need to scaffold the virtual experience with periodic small-group and whole-class discussion to reduce eye strain and dizziness. For example, students could locate their favorite exhibit and describe what they recall about it to a classmate. Alternatively, the teacher could send the students on a virtual scavenger hunt to find multiple exhibits throughout the museum, which may aid in the recall of the in-person experience. As virtual reality technologies continue to advance and become more ubiquitous in classrooms and everyday life, this issue may recede.

Equity Issues Related to Virtual-Reality Field Trips

Fewer students are having the opportunity to participate in field trips as part of their K–12 experience due to financial and time constraints as well as issues like a pandemic. Many participants perceived virtual field trips as an alternative for those who could not go on in-person field trips, including underserved students (Harron et al., 2019). This circumstance raises two important questions: Could the use of virtual field trips reproduce educational inequities that are already present in the system? Furthermore, could the use of virtual field trips unintentionally justify the lack of access to in-person field trips, particularly with underserved populations?

At the moment, the cost of implementing virtual field trips with an entire class continues to be high when compared to in-person field trips. As student ownership of smartphones and affordable class sets of devices increase, however, virtual field trips may become more common in the education system. Moving forward, proactive steps should be taken to ensure that this technology is not used to justify, replicate, and widen existing disparities. As such, we reiterate that the Harron et al. (2019) study used virtual-reality field trips in conjunction with an in-person field trip experience, not as a replacement.

Cloud-Based Computing—NetLogo in a Cloud-Based Environment

One of the projects we are excited about is the Group-Based Cloud Computing for STEM Education Project, which demonstrates how novel learning technologies can enhance PBI. This program has been funded by the National Science Foundation and utilizes iteration to design, develop, implement, and study a sociotechnological system for group-centered STEM teaching and learning. The system consists of the following:

- A flexible set of communications technologies provide a network infrastructure that can be deployed reliably and robustly in classrooms, even when the surrounding school network is unreliable.
- An integrated array of representation technologies supports data-rich collaborative learning in specific STEM disciplines.
- A suite of research-based collaborative activities deploys the representation and communications infrastructure for group-level learning in the tradition of generative design.
- A powerful approach to teacher education and preparation (UTeach STEM) marries training in STEM disciplines with practical and theoretical questions of classroom instruction.
- An instrumentation plan produces data about classroom interactions with the emerging system, both in elementary and secondary classrooms in the field and in classrooms within the UTeach program, to drive cycles of design-based research.

Two of the principal investigators on this project were cofounders of the UTeach STEM program. Three of the principal investigators have been actively involved in the design and development of technology components of the system in both research and corporate settings, as well as in study of teacher practices with group-centered teaching and learning at small and large scales. The project addresses the following questions:

1. How can the integrated group-based cloud computing environment be shown to be capable of supporting participatory and more fully socially mediated forms of classroom activity through use in an innovative, STEM-focused preservice program?
2. Can we develop ways of understanding how teacher capacity building presents a credible strategy for transforming student understanding and potential career trajectories by attending to what issues are raised, and how they are addressed, relative to the implementation of innovation both of the specific sort advanced in this project but also, plausibly, in support of attempts to introduce similar group-oriented, technological innovations in STEM education?

As part of our pursuit of design-based research intended to advance the state of the art in innovative, open, and cloud-based technologies for group-based learning and teaching, the integration with the nationally recognized UTeach STEM certification program plays an important role. Rather than encouraging teachers to simply "add on" domain-specific use of technology to their existing practices, the UTeach STEM certification program looks to "build in" the use of innovative STEM technologies as part of the students' certification program so that these future teachers are both prepared and experienced in integrating technology as part of their day-to-day pedagogical practices. Design-based research efforts focused primarily on elementary preservice teachers enrolled in a science methods course as well as junior and senior secondary preservice teachers enrolled in UTeach's capstone Project-Based Instruction course.

Example: Using Group-Based Cloud Computing to Understand Ecological Systems

The course Project-Based Instruction in the UTeach Program is offered to students as they are finishing their undergraduate careers. Preservice teachers enrolled in this course engage in the theoretical underpinnings of PBI, plan and execute a 3-day teaching experience at a local high school, and design a full Project-based unit. In the final weeks of the semester, the instructor (Max Sherard) wanted to provide preservice teachers with an opportunity to engage with computer-based models to elicit ideas of how these models could be used in PBI. Eight PBI students enrolled in the course engaged in a 90-minute lesson where they (a) watched the anchor video, "How Wolves Change Rivers"; (b) explored standards-based lessons related to food webs and ecology; (c) explored computer models involving wolves, elk, and aspen trees; and (d) discussed implications of using collaborative modeling in their future classrooms. The models used in the lesson were modified versions of the wolf-sheep predation model, edited by undergraduate computer science student Mica Kohl. In Version 1 of Kohl's modified model, she changed the sheep from the original model to an elk figure to match the video. In Version 2 of Kohl's modified model, she included parameters that show overgrazing occurring as a spectrum, rather than a binary (grass/no-grass). PBI students were excited to engage with the models and had many ideas of how these models can aid learners in developing a complex and quantified understanding of how populations shift over time with regard to their ecological relationships—a development that standards-based lessons often fail to achieve.

Example: Using Group-Based Cloud Computing to Understand Segregation

Framed through the lens of complex behaviors in systems (Jacobson et al., 2016), we also developed a lesson focused on how behaviors of individual agents in a system can lead to complex emergent results. Based on the Schelling (1971) model of racial segregation, the PBI class was invited to explore segregation as an emergent phenomenon using agent-based modeling. By adjusting a variable called "happiness," circles and squares move around a map until they are surrounded by a user-defined minimum percentage of neighbors who were the same as them. Students can adjust the minimum percentage and run the model multiple times to test different hypotheses about how the preference for similarity may result in different segregation patterns.

The lesson then turned to maps to provide a localized context for how segregation historically has occurred in Austin, Texas. Through reading about the history of Austin and viewing maps, students learned that the neighborhood of Hyde Park was originally developed for Whites only, that in the 1930s the Home Owners Loan Corporation labeled African American and Latino/a neighborhoods as "hazardous," and that over the past three decades the African American population of East Austin has become increasingly displaced by White residents. This investigation led to conversations based on three questions:

1. How are these maps of Austin related to deliberate segregation?
2. How are these maps of Austin related to circumstantial segregation?
3. Why is understanding this history relevant in conversations about systemic education reform?

Following this discussion, students investigated maps coded by race to take a look at how segregation takes place in Austin and metropolitan and rural areas throughout the United States. Other students looked at their home city or towns, with one student commenting that their rural experience was represented almost completely by those identifying as White. Returning to the group-based cloud computing model, the discussion on segregation culminated with three additional questions:

1. What does this agent-based model do well? Not so well?
2. Does this segregation model fairly represent how segregation takes place in Austin? Why or why not?
3. How can modeling be used to better understand the challenges in systemic education reform?

This lesson provided an introduction to how agent-based modeling can be used in a classroom to model and facilitate discussion about social issues in an immediate and localized context. Students were left with the challenge to think about how models and simulations can be used as a tool to address systemic education reform in the context of PBI. Such modeling activities offer rich possibilities for using technology to support students' Project work.

PBI AND ISSUES OF EQUITY, DIVERSITY, AND ACCESS

PBI as an Avenue for Equity

PBI offers powerful opportunities for students to build 21st-century skills; to engage in learning activities that are rigorous and relevant; to learn while making connections between subject areas and skills needed in college and careers; to use technology for communication, collaboration, and learning; and to engage in partnerships with community institutions and local stakeholders (Lee & Galindo, 2018). PBI involves students identifying a need or problem; identifying and choosing possible solutions; creating, running, and inspecting a particular solution; and then reflecting back. This differs from traditional forms of instruction that can involve students solving closed-ended problems where they rotely and passively apply a given procedure, with little need for collaboration and meaningful discussion given the sparseness of the tasks and without realistic reasons or larger purposes as a motivator for solving problems. Approaches of this type have been referred to as the "pedagogy of poverty" (Haberman, 1991).

Importantly, each approach prepares students for different kinds of futures. Students who experience only traditional instruction are taught to follow someone else's procedures without necessarily understanding them; to do repetitive, simple tasks with no larger purpose behind them; to work individually; and to obey authority. PBI, conversely, can prepare students to confront complex tasks through collaboration, productive struggle, inventiveness, creative problem-solving, and constructive cycles of feedback and revision. One could imagine the types of jobs in our society that utilize each set of skills. A commitment to equity and access for underserved students requires acknowledging that traditional instruction has served a social purpose of preventing mobility to different kinds of jobs and futures, whereas PBI, if done well, has the potential to open up STEM to a far more diverse set of thinkers and doers.

An important question, then, is what the research actually says about the impact of PBI on traditionally underserved students. Woods and Walkington (2020) reviewed 24 peer-reviewed studies (published 2007–2019) of PBI in Grades 6–12. Their search terms focused on PBI approaches integrated across STEM fields, and 20 of the 24 reviewed studies focused on underserved students. Some studies in their review provided evidence of the positive effect PBI can have on STEM achievement (Cogger & Miley, 2012; Cwikla et al., 2014; Erdogan et al., 2016; Foutz et al., 2011; Han et al., 2016; Hansen & Gonzales, 2014; Harris et al., 2015; Knezek et al., 2013; Lynch et al., 2017). Additional reviewed studies showed the potential of PBI to cultivate 21st-century skills (Bass et al., 2016; Cho & Brown, 2013; Lynch et al., 2017) and to improve attitudes towards STEM (Beckett et al., 2016; Cwikla et al., 2014; Knezek et al., 2013; Lynch et al., 2017; Mohr-Schroeder et al., 2014; Mosley et al., 2010; Redmond et al., 2011; Sahin & Top, 2015; Verma et al., 2011; Wilson et al., 2018).

The Woods and Walkington (2020) review also examined the key characteristics of PBI that supports underserved students. They found that students should have access to authentic real-world project experiences. Teachers should have opportunities to integrate across STEM subjects, to integrate technology as a tool for learning, to use student-centered instructional strategies focused on STEM habits of mind, and to involve community partnerships. They also pointed out the importance of school culture and teachers implementing PBI. Finally, the review identified supports teachers in these settings need to successfully implement PBI. Long-term, sustained professional development and opportunities for collaboration through professional learning communities were important to teachers' success.

Enacting high-quality PBI in underserved schools can be an important driver of social justice, but it is important to point out that students themselves can become agents of social change through PBI. The Projects students work on and the driving questions students confront can explicitly involve social justice themes and ideas relevant to students and their communities—such as racial profiling, the closing of "underperforming" schools, gentrification, school overcrowding, economic inequality, environmental justice, and climate change (Gutstein & Peterson, 2013). In the remainder of this section, we explore the relationship between local social issues and PBI.

PBI and Opportunities for Service Learning

Service learning is an important opportunity related to PBI to promote equity and access. With its emphasis on learning through participation in, service to, and collaboration with the broader community, the service-learning pedagogy would posit that at least one of the purposes of education is to promote citizenship and civic responsibility. Indeed, the philosophical underpinnings of the service-learning philosophy bears a strong resemblance to that of the social meliorist curriculum movement of the 1930s, which viewed education and schools as vehicles to address the ongoing social and economic problems of society by raising up a new generation of students critically attuned to social problems and prepared to address these issues (Kliebard, 2004). Initiatives include the National and Community Service Act of 1990 and National and Community Service Trust Act of 1993, as well as national, state, and private sector programs and organizations such as the national Serve America Program, national Learn and Serve America Program, and private-sector Learning in Deed (Furco & Billig, 2002). Clearly, this commitment to cultivating civic activism among American youth has long been a national ideal and value intimately linked to some of the core principles of democracy upon which American society is built.

Service learning is a pedagogy and a philosophy deeply rooted in constructivist and sociocultural theories of learning, as Pritchard and Whitehead (2004) explained:

> The connections between these propositions from constructivist learning theory and service-learning are readily apparent. Service-learning engages students in interacting with the world and thus helps them build new cognitive structures in accord with Piaget's general view of intellectual development. It involves students in collaborative work with teachers, peers and community members and thus engages them in the dialogic social interaction identified by Vygotsky as crucial to intellectual maturation. (p. 7)

Despite its long history in American society and the vast literature surrounding it, one would be hard pressed to find a singular definition of service learning (Swanson et al., 2014), a task further complicated by various terms to denote service learning (Bielefeldt & Pearce, 2012; Swanson et al., 2014). Nevertheless, Bielefeldt and Pearce (2012) offered a useful operative definition of service-learning:

> a course-based, credit-bearing, educational experience in which students (a) participate in an organized service activity that meets identified community needs and (b) reflect on the service activity in such a way as to gain further understanding of course content, a broader appreciation of the discipline, and an enhanced sense of civic responsibility. (p. 24)

With its emphasis on the linkage of curricular goals to address the authentic needs of a community partner and in collaboration with them, service learning can be an embodiment of Deweyan principles of learn by doing and experiential learning (Bringle & Hatcher, 2009; Payne, 2000; Pritchard & Whitehead, 2004). As such, service learning easily becomes an enriching complement to, or is perhaps even best realized in, similar constructivist pedagogies like PBI. The service-learning literature often discusses service learning in the context of project-based service learning.

Research has shown that situating learning around real problems and within authentic contexts, as is typical of PBI, can have some important implications for deep learning. For example, Stolk and Harari (2014), as well as Holmes and Hwang (2016), found compelling quantitative and qualitative evidence highlighting student motivation in a PBI setting as being a strong predictor of elaboration skills, critical thinking, and other cognitive strategies. This was, in large part, due to the real-world contexts featured in the PBI units (Holmes & Hwang, 2016). Other scholars have found similar findings and espoused the need for authentic project contexts (Kuhn et al., 2017). The advantages afforded by authentic project contexts thus make project-based service learning a particularly compelling approach to PBI. Project-based service learning enhances this notion of an authentic context and a real, meaningful problem by fundamentally requiring students to deeply learn the necessary skills and knowledge to address a real community need. That is, the authentic context and meaningful problem are provided through the community partner to be served in a project-based service-learning unit. In these ways and more, project-based service learning is a pedagogy that holds much potential to radically transform American education. Educators are challenged to be more deliberate in the design of learning experiences such that students may learn in realistic and relevant contexts that also promote a sense of civic duty and social purposefulness.

Local Social Issues in PBI

Service learning is an important example of how PBI can be community centered. However, additional kinds of opportunities for community engagement exist. The future of PBI in K–12 STEM education is dependent upon changes to preservice teacher education. Furthermore, changes to preservice teacher education must be met with new partnerships between academic and professional STEM organizations and local community organizations. In this section, we discuss the involvement of local social issues in the problem definition, formation of driving questions, and audience selection in PBI.

An important element of PBI that promotes equity, diversity, and access involves the locus of Projects. Many successful and researcher-documented Projects have involved engaging learners in thinking about macroscopic scientific problems. For example, some Projects have had learners plan for a simulated space trip to Mars or model the global trends in carbon dioxide emissions and create a mitigation strategy. Whereas projects involving macroscopic scientific problems are important, they can accidentally perpetuate a narrative where STEM applications have relatively little to do with day-to-day lived experiences. This wedge between people's lived experiences and the work of STEM could be related to public distrust in STEM.

One possible future direction (and solution) is to develop Projects based on local social issues. PBI centered on local social issues, particularly social inequity and injustice, could demonstrate the need for the tools of STEM to be appropriated and applied to problems that people experience in their day-to-day lives. For example, ongoing work with preservice STEM teachers currently enrolled in a PBI course involves using computational models and online mapping software to explore local neighborhoods and evaluate spaces for urban heat island effect. Preservice teachers are paying particular attention to areas of the city that experience higher than average temperatures due to features of the built environment and are exploring how these differences affect people based on socioeconomics and race. Recentering PBI on local social issues also provides an opportunity to involve local experts and community members in the role of the authentic audience. By bringing together local community experts with teachers, students, and STEM experts, we can lessen the gap between professional STEM and people's lived experiences.

CLOSING THOUGHTS: WHERE DO WE GO FROM HERE?

Looking past uncertainty in the present makes predictions about the future all the more difficult. Fortunately, the power of PBI lies in the innate opportunities to model and use the tools and skills needed to deal with uncertainty, particularly when PBI is driven through inquiry as the focus for exploring the unknown and unfamiliar. The challenges facing our world are substantial, ranging in medical, political, philosophical, and technological areas and more, but those challenges are not insurmountable. As society navigates multiple simultaneous global catastrophes, we are charging teachers with a call to help their students dig deeper into developing the underlying foundational skills they need to facilitate PBI with high leverage. Those skills include communicating, collaborating, critical thinking, developing a strong work ethic, and learning how to advocate for self and others. Our challenges may be great, but helping each other learn and grow can help us transcend the issues we face now and prepare us as we forge ahead into the future.

REFERENCES

Bass, K. M., Hu Dahl, I., & Panahandeh, S. (2016). Designing the game: How a project-based media production program approaches STEAM career readiness for underrepresented young adults. *Journal of Science Education and Technology*, 25(6), 1009–1024. https://doi.org/10.1007/s10956-016-9631-7

Beckett, G. H., Hemmings, A., Maltbie, C., Wright, K., Sherman, M., & Session, B. (2016). Urban high school student engagement through CincySTEM iTEST projects. *Journal of Science Education and Technology*, 25(6), 995–1007. http://doi.org/10.1007/s10956-016-9640-6

Behrendt, M., & Franklin, T. (2014). A review of research on school field trips and their value in education. *International Journal of Environmental and Science Education, 9*(3), 235–245.

Bielefeldt, A. R., & Pearce, J. M. (2012). Service learning in engineering. In T. H. Colledge (Ed.), *Convergence: Philosophies and pedagogies for developing the next generation of humanitarian engineers and social entrepreneurs* (pp. 24–52). NCIIA. https://digitalcommons.mtu.edu/materials_fp/54/

Bringle, R. G., & Hatcher, J. A. (2009). Innovative practices in service-learning and curricular engagement. *New Directions For Higher Education, 2009*(147), 37–46. https://doi.org/10.1002/he.356

Cho, Y., & Brown, C. (2013). Project-based learning in education: Integrating business needs and student learning. *European Journal of Training and Development, 37*(8), 744–765. http://doi.org/10.1108/EJTD-01-2013-0006

Cogger, S. D., & Miley, D. H. (2012). Model wind turbine design in a project-based middle school engineering curriculum built on state frameworks. *Advances in Engineering Education, 3*(2), 1–23. https://advances.asee.org/wp-content/uploads/vol03/issue02/papers/aee-vol03-issue02-p07.pdf

Cwikla, J., Milroy, S., Reider, D., & Skelton, T. (2014). Pioneering Mars. *The American Biology Teacher, 76*(5), 300–305. https://doi.org/10.1525/abt.2014.76.5.2

Erdogan, N., Navruz, B., Younes, R., & Capraro, R. M. (2016). Viewing how STEM project-based learning influences students' science achievement through the implementation lens: A latent growth modeling. *EURASIA Journal of Mathematics, Science & Technology Education, 12*(8), 2139–2154. http://doi.org/10.12973/eurasia.2016.1294a

Falk, J. H., & Dierking, L. D. (2016). *The museum experience revisited.* Routledge.

Falk, J. H., Martin, W. W., & Balling, J. D. (1978). The novel field-trip phenomenon: Adjustment to novel settings interferes with task learning. *Journal of Research in Science Teaching, 15*(2), 127–134. https://doi.org/10.1002/tea.3660150207

Foutz, T., Navarro, M., Hill, R. B., Thompson, S. A., Miller, K., & Riddleberger, D. (2011). Using the discipline of agricultural engineering to integrate math and science. *Journal of STEM Education: Innovations and Research, 12*(1–2), 24–32.

Furco, A., & Billig, S. H. (Eds.). (2002). *Service-learning: The essence of the pedagogy.* Information Age.

Gutstein, E., & Peterson, B. (Eds.). (2013). *Rethinking mathematics: Teaching social justice by the numbers* (2nd ed.). Rethinking Schools.

Haberman, K. (1991). The pedagogy of poverty versus good teaching. *Phi Delta Kappan, 73*(4), 290–294. https://doi.org/10.1177/003172171009200223

Han, S., Capraro, R. M., & Capraro, M. M. (2016). How science, technology, engineering, and mathematics project based learning affects high-need students in the U.S. *Learning and Individual Differences, 51*, 157–166. https://doi.org/10.1016/j.lindif.2016.08.045

Hansen, M., & Gonzalez, T. (2014). Investigating the relationship between STEM learning principles and student achievement in math and science. *American Journal of Education, 120*(2), 139–171. https://doi.org/10.1086/674376

Harris, C. J., Penuel, W. R., D'Angelo, C. M., DeBarger, A. H., Gallagher, L. P., Kennedy, C. A., Cheng, B. H., & Krajcik, J. S. (2015). Impact of project-based curriculum materials on student learning in science: Results of a randomized controlled trial. *Journal of Research in Science Teaching, 52*(10), 1362–1385. https://doi.org/10.1002/tea.21263

Harron, J. R., Petrosino, A. J., & Jenevein, S. (2019). Using virtual reality to augment museum-based field trips in a preservice elementary science methods course. *Contemporary Issues in Technology and Teacher Education, 9*(4), 687–707.

Holmes, V., & Hwang, Y. (2016). Exploring the effects of project-based learning in secondary mathematics education. *Journal of Educational Research, 109*(5), 449–463. https://doi.org/10.1080/00220671.2014.979911

Howitt, C. (2007). Pre-service elementary teachers' perceptions of factors in an holistic methods course influencing their confidence in teaching science. *Research in Science Education, 37*(1), 41–58. https://doi.org/10.1007/s11165-006-9015-8

Jacobson, M. J., Kapur, M., & Reimann, P. (2016). Conceptualizing debates in learning and educational research: Toward a complex systems conceptual framework of learning. *Educational Psychologist, 51*(2), 210–218. https://doi.org/10.1080/00461520.2016.1166963

Kazempour, M., & Sadler, T. D. (2015). Pre-service teachers' science beliefs, attitudes, and self-efficacy: A multi-case study. *Teaching Education, 26*(3), 247–271. https://doi.org/10.1080/10476210.2014.996743

Kisiel, J. (2013). Introducing future teachers to science beyond the classroom. *Journal of Science Teacher Education, 24*(1), 67–91. https://doi.org/10.1007/s10972-012-9288-x

Kliebard, H. M. (2004). *The struggle for the American curriculum: 1893–1958* (3rd ed.). RoutledgeFalmer.

Knezek, G., Christensen, R., Tyler-Wood, T., & Periathiruvadi, S. (2013). Impact of environmental power monitoring activities on middle school student perceptions of STEM. *Science Education International, 24*(1), 98–123.

Kuhn, D., Arvidsson, T. S., Lesperance, R., & Corprew, R. (2017). Can engaging in science practices promote deep understanding of them? Science practices. *Science Education, 101*(2), 232–250. https://doi.org/10.1002/sce.21263

Lee, J., & Galindo, E. (Eds.). (2018). *Rigor, relevance, and relationships: Making mathematics come alive with project-based learning*. National Council of Teachers of Mathematics.

Lynch, S. J., Spillane, N., House, A., Peters-Burton, E., Behrend, T., Ross, K. M., & Han, E. M. (2017). A policy-relevant instrumental case study of an inclusive STEM-focused high school: Manor New Tech High. *International Journal of Education in Mathematics, Science and Technology, 5*(1), 1–20. http://doi.org/10.18404/ijemst.75656

Metz, D. (2005). Field based learning in science: Animating a museum experience. *Teaching Education, 16*(2), 165–173. https://doi.org/10.1080/10476210500122733

Mohr-Schroeder, M. J., Jackson, C., Miller, M., Walcott, B., Little, D. L., Speler, L., Schooler, W., & Schroeder, D. C. (2014). Developing middle school students' interests in STEM via summer learning experiences: See Blue STEM Camp. *School Science and Mathematics, 114*(6), 291–301. https://doi.org/10.1111/ssm.12079

Morentin, M., & Guisasola, J. (2015). The role of science museum field trips in the primary teacher preparation. *International Journal of Science & Mathematics Education, 13*(5), 965–990. https://doi.org/10.1007/s10763-014-9522-4

Mosley, P. H., Liu, Y., Hargrove, S. K., & Doswell, J. T. (2010). A pre-engineering program using robots to attract underrepresented high school and community college students. *Journal of STEM Education: Innovations and Research, 11*(5–6), 44–54.

Payne, D. A. (2000). *Evaluating service-learning activities & programs.* Scarecrow Press.

Pritchard, F. P., & Whitehead, G. I. (2004). *Serve and learn: Implementing and evaluating service-learning in middle and high schools.* Erlbaum.

Redmond, A., Scott, M., Thomas, J., Jordan, P., High, K., & Dockers, J. (2011). Enriching science and math through engineering. *School, 11*, 399–408. https://doi.org/10.1111/j.1949-8594.2011.00105.x

Sahin, A., & Top, N. (2015). STEM Students on the Stage (SOS): Promoting student voice and choice in STEM education through an interdisciplinary, standards-focused, project based learning approach. *Journal of STEM Education, 16*(3), 24–34. https://www.jstem.org/jstem/index.php/JSTEM/article/view/1911/1683

Schelling, T. C. (1971) Dynamic models of segregation. *Journal of Mathematical Sociology, 1*, 143–186. https://doi.org/10.1080/0022250X.1971.9989794

Stolk, J., & Harari, J. (2014). Student motivations as predictors of high-level cognitions in project-based classrooms. *Active Learning in Higher Education, 15*(3), 231–247. https://doi.org/10.1177/1469787414554873

Swanson, C., Paterson, K., & Bielefeldt, A. R. (2014). Community engagement in engineering education as a way to increase inclusiveness. In A. Johri & B. M. Olds (Eds.), *Cambridge handbook of engineering education research* (pp. 283–309). Cambridge University Press.

Verma, A. K., Dickerson, D., & McKinney, S. (2011). Engaging students in STEM careers with project-based learning—MarineTech Project. *Technology and Engineering Teacher, 71*(1), 25–31.

Walkington, C., Gravell, J., & Huang, W. (2021). Using virtual reality during remote learning to change the way teachers think about geometry, collaboration, and technology. *Contemporary Issues in Technology and Teacher Education, 21*(4). https://citejournal.org/volume-21/issue-4-21/general/using-virtual-reality-during-remote-learning-to-change-the-way-teachers-think-about-geometry-collaboration-and-technology

Wilson, R. T., Watson, E., Kaelin, M., & Huebner, W. (2018). Early preparation and inspiration for STEM careers: Preliminary report of the epidemiology challenge randomize intervention, 2014–2015. *Public Health Reports, 133*(1), 64–74. https://doi.org/10.1177/0033354917746983

Woods, D., & Walkington, C. (2020). The evidence base behind the UTeach capstone course: Does project-based learning work? In J. Goodell & S. Koç (Eds.), *Preparing STEM teachers: The UTeach replication model* (pp. 241–258). Information Age Publishing.

ABOUT THE AUTHORS

Anthony J. Petrosino is emeritus at The University of Texas at Austin. He has received over 25 million dollars in grants from the National Science Foundation, the Department of Education and the McDonnel Foundation for Cognitive Studies. His research interests include students' understanding of experimentation, engineering education and the development of expertise. He is co-founder of the nationally recognized UTeach Program. Versions of his original course on Project-Based Instruction first taught in 2000 are now taught in 45 colleges and universities around the United States. He is currently a Professor of the Learning Scientist at Southern Methodist University. He received his PhD at Vanderbilt University where he was a member of the Cognition and Technology Group at Vanderbilt (CTGV). While doing his doctoral work, Petrosino was a NASA Space Grant Fellow funded through the Department of Mechanical Engineering. Petrosino was also a post-doctoral fellow at the Wisconsin Center for Educational Research and holds a master's degree in educational administration from Teachers College, Columbia University. Petrosino taught secondary science for seven years and is a certified K–12 teacher of science. In addition, he was an assistant superintendent of schools and was also a secondary school administrator. Dr. Petrosino has published over 40 peer reviewed journal articles, made over 100 national and international conference presentations, and has supervised a dozen doctoral dissertations. His articles have appeared in the *Journal of Science Education and Technology, The Journal of the Learning Sciences, Mathematical Thinking and Learning, Educational Computing Research, The Journal of Engineering Education*, and The *American Educational Research Journal*.

Candace Walkington is a Professor in Teaching and Learning at Southern Methodist University, specializing in mathematics education and learning sciences. Dr. Walkington's research examines how abstract mathematical ideas can become connected to students' concrete, everyday experiences such that they become more understandable. She conducts research on "personalizing" mathematics instruction to students' out of-school interests and also examines ways to connect mathematical practices with physical motions including gestures. Her work examines new technologies for STEM learning such as motion capture, Augmented Reality, Virtual Reality, game-based learning, and adaptive learning through Artificial Intelligence. She received the Presidential Early Career Award for Scientists and Engineers (PECASE) from the White House. Dr. Walkington has worked with the UTeach secondary math and science teacher preparation program at the University of Texas at Austin, and currently teaches courses for preservice and in-service mathematics teachers at Southern Methodist University.

Denise Ekberg, beginning in 2006 began work with the UTeach Natural Sciences program as a Clinical Assistant Professor. She has worked with new teacher Induction, and taught Student Teaching Seminar, Step 1—Intro to Teaching Math and Science Elementary School, Step II—Intro to Teaching Math and Science Middle School and Project-Based Instruction. Denise has also taught Research Methods. She has traveled with the UTeach French Exchange program as well as visited Universities that are replicating the UTeach program. Denise received her BS in biochemistry from the University of California at Davis and MS in biochemistry from the University of Illinois at Champaign/Urbana. Prior to teaching, she pursued research topics in plant genetics, drug delivery systems, cholesterol and lipid biochemistry and protein transport in mitochondria. Denise began teaching high school in 1990 as an inaugural corps member of Teach for America. She taught biology, chemistry, and AP chemistry in New Orleans for 15 years.